S0-ACQ-452

The Snake

velvet

THE SNAKE
Melanie Desmoulins
ISBN 1 871592 82 8
A Velvet Book
Copyright © S. Ahmed, 1997
Melanie Desmoulins asserts her moral right to be recognised as author of this work
First edition 1997
Copyright © Velvet Publications 1997
All rights reserved
Published by
VELVET PUBLICATIONS
83 Clerkenwell Road
London EC1, UK
T: 0171-430-9878
F: 0171-242-5527
E: velvet@pussycat.demon.co.uk
A Bondagebest Production

Design:
Bradley Davis, PCP International
Cover photograph:
Copyright © Richelle Simpson-Little 1997
Author's acknowledgments:
Thanks to Lucy

To my soul

*The Master of the Universe has bestowed upon them
the empire of seduction*
—Shaykh Nefzawi, *The Perfumed Garden*

The snake lay waiting. Coiled.

.

one

The whore was hot
Hot. The red cavern of her cunt
Hot. The taut marbles of her nipples
Hot. The firm inner thighs ready to clasp
She would have her tongue ready
She would have her friction-burned knees
Ready
Man or woman
It didn't matter
She would take either
Or both
And lead them up to heaven
And down to hell
Following the slithering path
Of the snake
She was in every woman
Who ever lived
She was in
Every tart
Every nun
Every housewife
Every worker
Every woman
That ever lived
In the bones of all
She yelled
Give me everything!
Give me all!

For I am you
And you are me
Nothing more
Nothing less
Together
We are
The perfect circle
The immaculate conception
The serpent's dream

δδδδδδδδδδδδ

The day was dead.

Lucy glanced up from her typewriter. The clock above the door said it was four. She got up.

"...leaving early today?"

Sandra's voice came from behind. Lucy did not turn around.

"Yes. It's in lieu."

"Have a nice weekend."

"Thanks. You, too."

"You doing anything?"

Lucy paused and thought. Then she wondered why she had paused. She would not be doing anything. There was never anything to do, any more. She should be used to that, by now. In her head, she ought to have grown accustomed to it.

"No – I'll probably just potter about."

As she went for her coat, she thought she saw Sandra turn towards Rita and the two of them smiled at each other but since this occurred at the very edge of her vision, she couldn't be sure. She wondered why she felt the compulsion always to be nice to everyone. They didn't seem to suffer from any such feeling towards her. Potter about, it sounded so bloody old. No, not bloody, at all. It was bloodless. Without passion. That was her, nowadays. It hadn't always been like that. But it was no good remembering the past. It only brought you sorrow. The sadness of missed opportunities. The melancholy of dead lovers.

She went into the Boss's office. He smiled at her as she entered. He was a small, bald, rounded man with a face like a tomato. He'd been good to her over the years. Never moaned when she was off. He was a good boss, as they went. But nowadays you couldn't trust anyone – not with jobs being like they were. He wasn't his own master – none of them were. She placed the sheaf of papers down on his desk.

"...the Brightwood orders. The first two quarters are summarized. I'll finish the last two on Monday."

He nodded.

"Looks like it'll be sodden at the races," he sighed.

A bachelor gambler, he wore only brown suits.

"Have a good weekend."

He glanced back down at his paperwork. As she closed the door, she imagined she detected a twinkle in his eye. Must've been the light, she mused. She stood before the mirror and adjusted her face. He'd never shown the slightest inclination towards her, she thought with a twinge of disappointment, but then why should he? He had money – not a fortune, but enough to be comfortable, to never have to worry about being out on the street, to go on holiday where he wanted. It didn't matter about the size of his prick, his chat-up lines, his lack of charm. Whether or not the thrusts of his loins were able to curry favour with the most feral of female beasts. The sort of bitches Lucy wanted desperately to be like. In spite of her moral upbringing, her polite exterior, somewhere deep inside the most hidden crevice of her cunt, she longed to have money and to be *loose*. At that moment, she pictured herself sucking cock – whose cock, she didn't care: his, maybe, anyone's, maybe – on the insides of her lips she felt the bulging veins which ran along the sides of every penile shaft, she tasted the pungent male secretion which adorned every male sex organ, she inhaled the stink of arousal, dog whore that she was; each breath an orgasm, every lick, a layering of stimulation. She'd been suffering from these fantasies recently – she wasn't sure, why, they had certainly never occurred during the entirety of her married life, Peter had always frowned upon such perverted, Eastern indulgences – Oh God! Sometimes she longed so hard for a hard cock, she would've killed – yes, killed, stripped the skin from a young cock's cock, torn the breasts from a virgin pubertal, sunk her incisors, dog-like, into the bulging scrotum of ten life-professed Dominican monks – for just the scent of a fuck. She'd seen the books, the filthy mags on their shelves and had wanted to buy one. Had wanted to be one of those naked, anus-pouting bitches in the camera's eye. Some of them were reputable, suburban wives: *Stacey from Chelmsford; Gillian from Birmingham; Janet from Glasgow*. How could they do it? What about the people they knew? Maybe they didn't know anyone. Maybe they didn't care. Perhaps their friends would envy them their splayed fame. Their vulval exposure. *f 100. Fuck 100. White leopard, Red pocket* – they had such corny names. And yet oh-so attractive. Enticing. *Nina de los Marchenas, Loucine Ohmeda, Susana Moreno*. Spanish-sounding, toros balls-sucking, cock-taut Spanish guitar-sounding names. She'd never ventured into the stores where they kept magazines just for women. Not in the High-street shops, those. You had to go underground for your first sight of a cock in rigor. A woman had to become a criminal, just to see and enjoy that which men could purchase along with the birthday cards and the sellotape. She knew where she might have obtained such 'literature'. Her work-mates had joked with her about it – *widow's weeds*, and all that. One day, Perhaps, she would venture along the road and buy herself that which she could not obtain by natural means... She forced the long thought into history so that she could make it into a long never-thought. She went back to the Boss. The Boss had money. He could have had his pick of women. Perhaps he did. Though she'd never actually seen him with anyone. He'd never made a pass at her. Not even a half-pass. She wondered if he might be gay. He didn't look gay – but then you never could tell, nowadays. *Damn!* She hated using that word, even to herself. *Nowadays*. It made her seem so ancient. Like one of those blue-rinse women everybody laughed at. She sighed, and her breath made an oval on the mirror. She stared at this imprint of her on glass. It faded from the centre out, so that an ever-thinning ring stood between her lips and the world beyond. It was an ever-vanishing vulva. Her vulva. She gazed, almost hypnotized by the changing form of the breath. They say the soul is like that, ever-changing and empty in the middle. Curling and coiling within.

The soul disappeared.

She inhaled. Anyway, who would want to go with a widow? She began to wipe the corners of her eyes. Not that she wore much make-up – not these days. Still, a woman had to look presentably smart, otherwise she'd be taken for a slob, or a slut, or something. She was proud of her smooth-skinned cheeks and her hair, still

Melanie Desmoulins

golden. She'd never smoked – that helped. Hardly drank, either. *No vices*, she thought. This made her laugh inside and her laugh spread faintly upon her wrinkleless cheeks like the touch of a breeze upon the face of a pond.

It was a wet winter's evening, the sort of murky end-day when she felt as though someone were constantly slipping ice-cubes down her back. She hated it. As she trudged to the bus-stop, Lucy glanced at the shop fronts without really looking. She'd had no interest in window-shopping since Peter died. She'd had no interest in anything. No, that wasn't true. There was her job. It had kept her sane during those dark days. You never knew what was going to hit you next. The rain began to sting her eyes. She wiped her hair off her face. So much for sorting herself out. She might as well not have bothered. Her umbrella would be useless on a day like this. The rain drove her back into her thoughts. Her work... yes, her work had given her what she'd needed most at the time. A sense of routine. Being routine. Boredom can be a saviour. In the days when she would go home to a house filled with emptiness, in a year of hollow days, all she'd had was her work. The typewriter was so utterly predictable with its lettered keys and its wonderful silence. Not that Jane wasn't helpful – she was – but she hadn't wanted to offload her own sorrow onto her daughter. She lived far away and anyhow, she'd had a hard enough time as it was, coping with her father's... death. She still found it hard to say, even after two-and-a-half years, one hundred-and-twenty weeks, seven hundred-and-twenty-three days. Each one, another breath away from Peter. She worried about Jane. She had no husband, no children. Didn't want either. Left home at eighteen. She'd had Jane when she was eighteen. Girls thought differently, nowadays. They had never forgiven each other for Peter's death. The traffic wound in coils of light around the buildings, trapping, throttling, suffocating...

Just then, as she passed by an alleyway, she saw a large bundle in a doorway. Then she realized the bundle consisted of a man and woman huddling together. They both wore long, dark overcoats and the woman was pressed against the door in the semi-darkness. They were giving each other long, deep, sensual kisses and although nearly all of their bodies were swathed in thick clothing, yet the centre of their being seemed to emanate from the union of their lips. Lucy felt her eye drawn to the soft pressure of

---

their desperation. The man's long tongue played around the woman's upper lip, then moved down to her fleshy lower lip. Their tongues met and played, before plunging deep into one another's mouths. Lucy felt her own mouth begin to water. It had been such a long time. The man thrust his hand beneath her dress which became suddenly hitched up at an indelicate angle. Lucy heard her moan softly as she let her head fall backwards against the door. The rain drove hard into Lucy's face, stinging her eyes but she did not dare blink. The woman's legs seemed to move apart like those of an ungainly doll. It seemed obscene somehow, to see a woman like that, fully-dressed with her legs spread. Sex was so utterly repulsive. And yet...

She could see clearly in the dark. She'd always been good at that. Sometimes, she was able to see even that which was invisible. She could feel the soft triangle of pink flesh, hidden enticingly in thick fur between the woman's legs. She felt it swell and burst with sticky sap. She sensed the heat of the male organ as it pulsated in the vertical. A church tower of a thing. Her palms tingled as the burning fire of its veins spread through the air. She could feel its rough walls even though she knew the woman had not yet touched it. The joy of delay. The snake-throat lust of post-ponement. The man's breath on her neck. The nip of teeth.

Delicious pain.

The figures had pushed further into the doorway, so that the woman was virtually hidden in darkness. But Lucy could still see the animal figures. She was able to make out the curves of flesh which define man and woman. No higher conceptions. Just base beast. The need of cunt to suck prick. The murderous desire. She would kill for it. She would eat the balls of any man to get what she wanted. Even Lucy. The secretary. The mother. The widow. She wasn't old. She was young and virile. She could take any man and fuck him senseless. She could make his cock need her, till he would die for a scent of her. That was the real her. That was inside all of the shell of civilisation. That was beneath the accretion of seven thousand years of bullshit words. No more words. Just a cunt and a cock. From the beginning of time to its pre-come end. She would fuck time itself. She would open up the penis-slit of the male god of time and she would make it fuck her mad. Or if it was a woman, she would suck its bulb till it was as large as the cock of a wrestler. She

Melanie Desmoulins

was with the woman in the doorway, the cunting whore of the city, earning her living in the cold rain. She was with the juices of sex, the only eternal commonality between one human being and the next. *Yes! Yes! Yes!* Lucy the woman, the female beast, was reborn at that moment. She would never die again. There was a glimpse of arched, white skin and then the man too, fell into shadow. The woman moaned again. The figures turned around. An awkward-shaped bundle emerged as the beasts drew up against one another in a different configuration, another debauchery. He was screwing her anus. Bumming her. Spewing his sperm-rich pre-come into her hot, wet shithole. She felt her own buttocks tauten. Pull together as if in anticipation. God! She was all fluid. *Woman is all water,* she thought. Lucy blinked.

The man caught Lucy's eye. A pale cheekbone. Yellow eyes. She ran.

As her blouse rubbed against her nipples, she realised they were berry-hard. Her breasts seemed to thrust out from beneath her overcoat like those of a woman in some old African print. She glanced around but no-one was following her. The street was unusually quiet, a hiatus in the midst of the crazy rush-hour. She slowed her pace and leaned against a wall. She felt a wetness between her thighs. There was a throbbing in her belly. Her breath came in hot rasps over her tongue, her lips. *Whore! Whore! Fucking Whore! People must think I'm mad,* she thought as she realised she had gone some hundred yards beyond her bus-stop. But then, she corrected herself, no-one would have noticed.

It was properly dark by the time she got home. An empty house. She'd thought of moving but hadn't had the courage. There were too many memories. Happy memories. Other memories. She wanted to keep them all. They belonged to her and to nobody else. No-one could take that away from her. Not even death itself. They were, what she was. She was the sum total of her past, and nothing more. They were pastel postcards of old sunny days. Sometimes, she hated that. Her ball-and-chain. There were times, usually in the depths of some rabid night, when she would gladly give away all of her past, everything...

It had been so long. Years. She hadn't even masturbated. Once she'd gone without for a certain time, it were as if she had traversed a threshold of some sort, the same watershed as that crossed by the Brides of Christ, sometime after their novitiate. Sex, and sexual desires, had receded into the background. Her own sex became less that an old photograph; no silver-gray mementos remained of passion, so that it became easy to imagine that it had hardly ever existed in the first place. When she thought about it, (which was pretty seldom), it seemed as though she were remembering some other woman's life, or reading some book she'd read once on a beach, a long time ago. The nights after she had been widowed, when the taper between her thighs would inflame and scorch her mercilessly, preventing sleep, had long gone. And anyway, after Peter had become ill, they had seldom done it. Never, in fact. And even before that, he hadn't exactly been a roaring lion of desire – not after the first year, at any rate – and she had incorporated his coldness into herself, wrapping lasciviousness in layer upon layer of daily life, until at length she no longer believed in its existence. A lie, she knew now. But it was too late. There was no point dwelling on it.

Tossing her sodden coat over the radiator, she went upstairs to wash her face and hands. Cold water brought her back to earth in seconds. It always did. It was a kind of instant Protestant purgatory. Soulless and quick. And without meaning. She brushed her long hair. It was still golden. She was proud of that. Usually, she would tie her hair back in a bob for work but the wind had unsettled it and so it flowed freely in gentle waves before the clear glass of the mirror. When she came back downstairs, she decided to make herself a good cup of tea. She flipped on the sitting-room light, revealing the pastel decor all around. Encircling. Someone had told her to re-decorate but what was the point. Who would it be for? Something caught the corner of her eye. Something white, on the dresser. She went over and picked it up. It was a letter. She got a knife to open it but then found it wasn't sealed. Folding back the unused, gummed edge, she pulled out the contents.

In her hand was a plane ticket and a travel agent's itinerary. Her first thought was that it had been put through the wrong letter-box. But there was her name on the envelope. Her name and her address. Well then, it must be someone else's ticket since she certainly hadn't booked any holiday. Why would she? But it was her name on the ticket and on the itinerary: *Lucy Thomas, Mrs.*

She began to study it in more detail. It was for four weeks

in Portugal, in the Algarve, at the Hotel Galicia. A town called Albernoa. The names sounded exotic, strangely compulsive beneath the electric light of her sitting-room. She felt a flame of excitement flicker in her chest and immediately forced it down and out. She was good at that. She'd had many years' practice at it.

A short note had been inserted into the envelope along with the tickets and itinerary. *To Mum, with love from Jane.*

So it was her.

She was unable to prevent a smile from easing its way across her tired skin. Then she pulled her face together. She couldn't possibly go. There was her work. She hadn't taken time off. How could Jane do this, without telling her? She didn't want to go on holiday, not now she was alone. What was the point? What would it achieve? She felt anger rising in her breast. Beside the dresser lay a case. Her case. She laid it down and flipped it open. It was full. Someone had packed it for her. She strode over to the phone and dialled her daughter's number. There was no reply. Just a hissing sound through the wires. She'd often wondered where all the voices went, after the ends of conversations. They went nowhere. Into oblivion. Like Peter. She forced the thought from her mind. She was about to replace the handset, when someone answered at the other end. A distant voice. Half her own.

"Hello?"

"Yes, it's Mum."

"Oh, hi..."

"Look, Jane, what's all this? It's all very good of you, I'm sure and I really appreciate it, really I do but I can't, I won't let you order my life like this. I won't go. I don't want..."

"Mum," Jane cut in.

"I don't need a hol..."

"Mum, listen. You're going and that's that."

"But..."

"Don't 'but' me. I'm beyond 'buts'. This is the first time I'm telling you to do anything, and you're going to do it."

Lucy felt the first stirrings of hope in her heart and instantly felt guilty.

"...But my work. I can't just drop everything and... they need me there."

"Don't worry."

"What do you mean, 'don't worry'? It's my job. I've had that job for the best part of twelve – no, more than twelve – years and..."

"I've spoken to your boss."

"...and I'm not... What! You did what!"

"I arranged it with your boss. He's got cover. They all knew at work – all except you. It was a surprise."

Jane paused. Lucy was lost for words.

"You've got four weeks off in the sun. Bye, Mum. Have a great time. You deserve it."

The phone went dead.

The hissing resumed, growing louder as the death of the phone grew deeper. Lucy slammed the handset down. For a while, the hissing continued in her ears, until at last it too, died away.

That night, Lucy dreamt of sex. It was the first time in years that she had allowed herself, even in her subconscious, to roam, naked and free over the unseen boundary which separates purest chastity from unremitting debauchery. In her dream, she was the alley-woman, the slut of a thousand dark nights. On some deeper level, in a dream beneath the dream, she knew that when she awoke in the morning, her sheets would bear the sticky witness to her guilt. The stains would never wash away.

Deep within the deepest black of the city, down the darkest of dark alleys, an ancient tramp crawled along the wet ground. From his mouth, there protruded a viper's tongue and the tongue was flicking in and out. His lips were dry and covered in scales and his eyes were yellow. He made low, grunting noises as he wound his way onwards along the alley. In the murky half-light, in the dank rainbeams of the bum-end of the day, the ten-layered tramp was following the line of silver to his salvation.

       Melanie Desmoulins

two

For us a female prophet has arisen;
Her laws we follow; for the rest of mankind
The prophets that appeared were always men.

The plane snaked its way across the ground while far below, in the cold villages and hot towns and deserted hills, acts took place in broad daylight which no devil could have imagined. Lovers stabbed one another in the heart, while men with horse-pricks stole like thieves along one another's backs. Sharp objects fell from arms and the bleeding trails which were left ran in streams down to the open mouth of the sea. The tart was growing larger between her legs, even as the man bulged desperately before her. She could make them want her till they died. She could make them want her till they were damned forever. She was the mistress of their desires, of their most secret dreams. She was the queen cunt of their moonlight longings. She would draw the milk from between the muscles of their thighs and would take it into herself. The warm, white slick of sex. The song of the ages. Every being's creation lay in that animal desire. Yes! We were all solely the result of a glorious fuck, and nothing more. Fuck till you die! And then fuck in Hell! Give us Hell, any day. For if the Devil gave us the screw, there must be more to him than meets the eye. He must be a fun bastard. No more of the sterility of saints. No more of flagellating nuns. No! No! No! Nothing matters more than the joining of one human being to another. Nothing. It over-rides everything, even survival. That's what every love tragedy was about. Sex over-arching everything. A great cock of a thing. A bursting flower of a paradise.

Even as she flew, Lucy felt herself sink. The fear of the

unfamiliar wound itself into a tight ball in the pit of her stomach. Nausea spread over her in a thick, green cloud. She felt out of place amongst all the loud, happy tourists. She felt guilty.

The Hotel Galicia was a medium-sized establishment of modern build. The staff were friendly, however and that made all the difference to Lucy. She just wanted a relaxing month by the sea. The moment she'd steeped from the airless cabin, the warm air had folded like a blanket around her body, she had relaxed and found it impossible not to want enjoy herself to the full. After all, there was nothing wrong with that. The guilt uncoiled in the shape of a dead skin from her body.

The ground floor was taken up with a spacious bar which surrounded a delicious, turquoise pool. Lucy liked to sit by the edge of the pool, sipping from a large *pina colada* or a long *blue lagoon* and watching the people as they sauntered by. On her second evening in Albernoa, a dark-haired woman in her late thirties sat down at the table next to her. She had skin which looked like it had been in the sun for years, if not forever, and a mouth that drooped slightly, in the manner of those old French paintings of courtesans. She looked like the sort of woman who'd just had a kinky fuck. She caught Lucy's eye and they both glanced away but then their eyes met again and the woman smiled. Lucy smiled back and remembered that she had seen her before, at breakfast. She had been speaking English with a slight Northern accent and had sported a long, cream cigarette from red-tipped nails. She had long, shiny black hair which swirled down around her cheeks in sensuous curves. Her eyes too, were black – so black, that Lucy was able to see her own reflection in their darkness. It were as if her whole body – her whole being – was in a state of incipient orgasm. Just at that moment, as she lit another pale brown cigarette. Lucy recalled wondering just how she could smoke so early in the day but since Lucy had given up years ago, she felt she was no expert to know, either way. Without warning, the woman got up and came to join Lucy.

"Might as well say hello!" she laughed, "I'm Rachel."

She proffered her hand. It was the sort of name which Lucy had been expecting. A slightly Jewish, slightly mysterious name. She wondered who the fuck had been with.

"Oh – yes. Um... Lucy. Lucy Thomas."

There was an awkward pause while neither woman seemed to know quite where to look. Just then, the waiter arrived with their orders.

"I noticed you at breakfast. Have you been here long... in the Algarve?"

"Only two days."

"How d'you like it?"

"It's nice. The weather is a change from London – especially at this time of year."

"Oh. Are you from London?"

Lucy nodded.

"You're from the North, aren't you?"

Rachel tipped the ash from her cigarette into a saucer.

"How did you know?"

"...Your accent."

"Oh, I thought I'd got rid of that, years ago! Been living in Surrey for ages. Till I moved here."

"You live here?"

Rachel sighed. Smoke poured from her nostrils. Lucy fought back the urge to grimace.

"Seven years, it's been."

Lucy expected her to go on, but she was silent. Not wishing to pry, Lucy asked her whether she had liked living in a foreign country. Rachel leaned forwards and spoke in a confidential tone. Lucy detected the slight odour of spirit on her breath, mixed in with the sickly perfume which lay dank upon her sun-tanned neck. And something else. Lucy shut this last sensation out. Denied it, as she had denied herself for so long.

"I'd never go back. Never. I've got everything anyone could ask for here – sun, sand, sea and..."

She paused.

"and..." Lucy prompted, forgetting her resolution not to pry. Rachel was far too interesting for her not to want to dig deeper. Besides, Lucy felt within herself the stirrings of envy.

"And men."

She said this with a dismissive wave, as if to say the men were something minor, something which she took for granted, perhaps something not to be relied upon. Lucy smiled and began to eat.

"I'll tell you about men," Rachel began. Lucy did not look up.

"I had a husband – back in England, you know, in Surrey. No kids, though. We had a good thing going. Huh! So I thought. Then he went off with a teenager. Bitch!"

"I'm sorry."

"Oh, don't be," she said with another wave of her hand. "The girl can't have had much of a fanny. She would've been just right for him."

Lucy winced but tried to hide it.

"When my mother died, I came into money. Not a fortune but enough to retire on, as it were."

"Retire? But you're only..."

There was a pause.

"How old do you think I am?"

"I...I don't know."

"Maybe I'm older than you think," she smiled and it was then that Lucy noticed some heavily-hidden crow's feet around the margins of her eyes and a faint puckering below the lids.

"Anyway, here I am. And here, I'll stay."

"Good for you."

Lucy noticed a slim young man dressed in a white suit approach their table. He had short, black hair rather in the style of the early Sixties. She quickly suppressed the thought, realising that it would show her age to be even thinking it. Rachel hadn't noticed him and continued to eat. He crept up behind her and tickled her suddenly beneath the arms. She jumped, almost spilling her drink.

"You! You..."

He planted a kiss on her neck. She closed her eyes and twisting herself around, she let her arms wrap themselves around his neck. Lucy pretended not to look.

"Antonio," Rachel announced as he proffered his hand. His grip was firm, his fingers warm as the sun. She felt his skin, smooth and tingling.

"Lucy... Lucy Watson," she stammered.

He must have been in his mid-twenties, she thought though people's ages seemed oddly obscure in this land of bright whites and deep blues. He topped six feet in height and had eyes of purest hazel. The sort of fire eyes you might fall into and quite happily

Melanie Desmoulins

burn in forever. It was easy to see why Rachel had fallen for him. She presumed she had.

"Lucy's from London, England."

"Ah, *Londres*. Good."

He clapped his hands together. They were tanned and smooth.

"I wanted to see London, always..."

"Don't be silly," Rachel slapped his hand playfully, "There's nothing to see there. Just rain and fools."

She paused.

"Oh I'm sorry, I didn't mean you, I was talking about the fools in my life. No offence, I hope."

"Of course not," Lucy smiled.

For the first time, he looked into her eyes. She glanced down.

"You have nice food here," she said, trying to change the subject.

"Chicken *piri-piri*. It's our national dish..."

"Antonio's a chef," Rachel cut in, "...well, an owner of chefs." She tossed her head, in the way that a mare might. Or a courtesan.

"I own the restaurants, not the chefs. I always say, Italian cuisine is the most healthy, French, the most varied, but Portuguese is the most passionate."

"Silly," Rachel swiped at his ear. He ducked and grinned, boyishly. He had a strong nose, the kind you could rely on, and finely-chiselled lips. His eyes were a rich brown. His hair was cropped in the continental style and his jaw was oval, as if he had once possessed a beard. Lucy decided then and there that she liked him better without it.

"Aren't you having something to eat?" Lucy asked. She tried not to sound too keen.

"Perhaps..." He caught her eye, then abruptly changed his mind.

"No, no. I'm far too busy."

"Busy? You're never busy."

He planted another kiss on Rachel's cheek. She kissed him back on the lips. She had bulbous lips. Used lips. It were as if Lucy was not there. As he walked away, Lucy struggled to tear her eyes away from his thighs which seemed ready to burst out from beneath his thin, white cotton trousers.

"Gorgeous, isn't he?" Rachel whispered.

Lucy nodded, slowly. She took a sip from the glass before her. Then she remembered. No, not remembered. She let it through. The scent. The smell which she had detected in the other woman's breath. It was the stink of male sex.

δδδδδδδδδδδδ

It was a golden day. The sea lay like a pane of glass beneath the deep blue sky. Lucy gazed upwards, shielding her eyes from the hot sun. It was only mid-February and yet the days were warm as a late Devon spring, though the nights were still chilly. Her fair skin was already beginning to peel and she splodged on another handful of Factor 20. She wasn't really sunbathing – she wasn't ready for that – rather, she'd sat herself down at a beachside café which she'd stumbled across quite by chance. Over to the right, lay the town of Albernoa with its old-style fishing boats and its walls cut in brilliant white. While over on her left were the newer resorts of Urra and Solveiro. A little of the old, a little of the new – she liked that. It was certainly better than the English winter. She's not been abroad much with Peter – he'd never really taken to foreign places, and certainly not to their food. She found herself quietly chuckling as she remembered this.

Then she stopped.

It must be the sangria, she mused. Still, it was good that she could laugh about the past. She hadn't done that in a long time. Ever. Perhaps Jane had been right – it would do her good to get away from it all, away from everybody. Living and dead. Funny, how the young could be right, sometimes. There I go again, she thought, a little irritated, calling myself old. I'm young, too. I'm young and attractive in a way that a bit-of-a-girl could never be. I have experience. I know what I like, and I know what a man wants. Yes, and I know what a woman likes, too. Because that's what I like. She giggled. The golden cliffs burned peacefully beneath the clean orb of the sun. Behind the cliffs, two young tourists were fucking. Lucy couldn't hear this, but she knew it was happening, in the same way she'd been able to see the coupling of the beasts in the alleyway back home. She chuckled at this. 'Back home'. What kind of home was London? A cold, frigid kind of place. She liked her passion out in the open. Exposed. *She liked Portugal. She drew its streaming heat to the pale curves of her body. She rubbed its olive oil smoothness between her legs. She let it violate her and leave her till the next time. The new Lucy. The old Lucy.* It was off-season. The pensioners were heading for home on their two- month tickets while the teenies and the families had not yet arrived – and would not come till Easter. A few people milled around on the small, enclosed beach while far out in the emptiness, the sea had the rocks all to itself.

Lucy finished her drink and got up. She wondered how she would get back to the road. She had arrived here by walking along the beach cliffs but didn't much fancy walking back all that way again. It was late afternoon and she wanted to lie down for a while. She asked the barman. He didn't seem to understand. Just kept saying:

"Taxi, taxi."

As if she could get a taxi here – there was no road.

"Look – I just want to get back to the road... my hotel – Hotel Galicia...?"

"...Galicia." He pointed towards the town in the far distance. The beach trailed on for an eternity.

"No, no. It's my hotel. Oh dear..."

Just then, a voice came from over her right shoulder.

"The way is up there – up by those rocks. It's a bit steep, but there is a path."

She spun round. It was Antonio.

"Um. I think he's having trouble understanding me. I only want to get to the road – I can walk from there. Or I could get a taxi..."

Antonio began to move off.

"It's this way," he motioned.

She hesitated, then thought, oh, what does it matter? I only want to find the road. This chap's being awfully helpful. One shouldn't be so paranoid. Besides, she liked his eyes.

The path was narrow and steep. Her silly beach shoes weren't really up to it. He had to help her around several hairpins. Suddenly, her foot slipped and she fell, grazing her knee on a rock.

"Oh dear, let me..." he said and helped her to her feet once again. His arms were bare and muscular and tanned darker than his face.

"Thanks," she said, brushing herself down.

"Oh – you've hurt your knee," he began.

She glanced down.

"It's nothing – just a graze. I'll be fine."

She gazed past him. "Is it this way?"

He smiled, ever so slightly.

She looked at him and the smile vanished. He turned around.

"Yes – this way. Not far to go, now."

They reached the road. There wasn't a car in sight. The heat rippled in waves along the smooth tarmac. Lucy began to feel a little giddy. His body was kind of... angular.

"Well – here it is. I think you'll have to walk. Not many taxis pass this way."

He paused and squinted in the sun. She looked straight at him. Those eyes, again. The colour of wine.

"Are you on holiday here?"

"Yes. For four weeks. It was a surprise... my daughter arranged it."

Why was she telling him this? He clapped his hands together, once.

"Delightful."

She thought he would go on, but he fell silent and began to gaze about him. Still, no car had passed them. Only an old man wearing a straw hat ached his way through the dust by the side of the road. Lucy wondered why he didn't walk on the tarmac.

"Doesn't look like you're in luck."

He seemed to decide something, there by the melting black river with the sea at his back.

"Look, Lucy – may I call you that – there's a little *cervejaria* across the road, just around the corner. Why don't we get something to drink? We can always phone for a taxi from there."

"Um... I don't know..."

She teetered on the brink. Why was he being so helpful? But

what choice had she? Anyway, she liked listening to him talk, she liked his voice, it was deep and warm and reminded her of an Algarve sunset, or a good glass of Brandymel.

"Alright. That's a good idea."

She began to walk.

"...This way?" she turned back and looked at him quizzically.

He smiled. That smile again. The lips just upturned at their ends in the shape of a crescent moon.

They sat at a table in the small cantina. His buttocks were rounded and firm. The kind any woman would die for. Looking at his muscular rump, she could feel the thrusts of which he would be capable.

"This is your first time in Algarve. I think."

She jerked her head up.

"...It's... it's my first time... actually, it's my first time abroad for years."

She paused. He must have sensed that she had something else to say, for he remained silent and simply gazed down into his glass, playing his finger around the rim.

"...My husband, Peter, he... he passed on two years ago, two-and-a-half years, actually. My daughter did this – booked this holiday for me. As a surprise."

"She must love you very much."

His eyes met hers. She glanced down. Now it was her turn to play with the glass.

"Yes, it was very hard. We'd been married for twenty-five years, you know."

She paused.

"It was cancer. It was very hard. I went on working – I work in an office – it kind of kept me going..."

He was nodding. His eyes had filled with feeling. Not compassion, not that exactly, but something else. She wasn't sure, what. His English was almost perfect. She wondered why she had lied to him.

"Can we phone for a taxi, Antonio?"

It was the first time she had called him by name.

"Yes, of course."

He got up. The sun blared like a loudspeaker across her face. He returned a few moments later.

"It will be here soon."

As they went out to the taxi, Antonio reached across and handed her bag to her.

"You forgot this."

She paused.

"Thankyou."

"*Obrigado.*"

"What?"

"*Obrigado.* It means 'thankyou'."

She laughed.

"Oh. *Obrigado.*"

They both laughed at her accent. The sun had grown louder and the ground basked in its voice. He inhaled deeply and then spoke quickly.

"What about dinner tonight? I know a place in town. It's really good. There's a singer... good food. Do me the honour."

Her head reeled. What was she doing? No, she couldn't. No, it was out of the question.

"That'd be fine," she smiled.

"Great!"

He brought his hands together, his big, warm hands and a smile broke out across his face like a great sunbeam across the sky.

"I'll pick you up at eight. What hotel were you staying at?"

"The Galicia. I met you there – remember?"

He nodded.

"I know it."

She wondered whether he had asked other women out to dinner from the same hotel.

"Eight."

As the yellow cab tore away and the Antonio figure shrank in the mirror, Lucy felt her heart pound as if it were going to burst. The sand swept in great swathes to the north and to the south. The colour of his neck.

For the first time in years, she sensed the thrill of a date. The trembling feeling in her chest. The sensation of death immanent. Joyous, glorious, unashamed death. She thought of his eyes and in them she saw herself. It seemed like another world, out here. She felt guilty as she realised her heart had dropped a beat.

O God! I'm wet she thought. Her fanny ached with desperate longing. *Give me a long, hot cock, long and burning and merciless, and I'll show you what I can do. Render unto me thy soul, and I'll take thee to hitherto unheard-of lands of joy and damnation. I want your long, sleek body, you bloody stud, I need the boiling gouts of your spunk inside me. I need it now! Please, please, please! Come and screw me. Come and fuck me. I will be your slave. I will be your mistress. I will be your moon goddess. I will be your all.*

three

Boil well in water carobs, freed from their kernels, and bark of the pomegranate tree. The woman takes a sitz bath in the decoction thus obtained, and which must be as hot as she can bear it; when the bath gets cold, it must be warmed and used again, and this immersion is to be repeated several times.

The whore was doing good business, that evening as she paraded yet again along the main street of Albernoa. Within her stinking cunt, she held captured the spunk of twelve men. A dozen children. She smiled as she thought of this. A man smiled back as he crossed the street and was sucked towards her long, buttocked frame. A great mother-goddess, she was. Mother to all fuckers. Every mother was a whore, and every whore, a mother. Lucy stood in the bathroom, gazing at herself in the full-length mirror. Her long, golden hair fell in waves down over her breasts. There were thin strands of silver strewn through the gold. They were hardly noticeable to anyone except herself. People had told her she ought to have it cropped short and business-like, saying it would take ten years off her. But she would never wear widow's weeds. She liked her hair – and what was wrong with that? Anyway, she was still young. Her skin was the colour of seashell. She ran her hands down over her flanks and buttocks and spun round, so that she would be able to view herself from over her shoulder. There was a little flab here and there, a little sag, perhaps – but not bad for her age. She perched up on her toes. She was five foot-four inches, five foot-six on heels. He must be at least six-two, she mused. A delicious tingle ran through her body as she sifted her hands over her thighs. She hadn't felt that for ages.

Not for ages.

Melanie Desmoulins

As the warm water washed down over her body, she felt guilt slide away from her with the dust and the grime. England was an age away. She spent time over her appearance, making sure her hair was exactly right, applying just the right amount of make-up. She didn't want him to think she was cheap. As she combed back her long, golden hair, she felt her body quiver, ever so slightly and she realized that her nipples were erect.

Antonio came for her in a sleek, white sports car that gleamed golden in the dying evening sun. He was wearing a cream open-necked shirt and a black dress jacket. As he got out, she saw that his matching trousers were pleated slightly at the top. Between the pleats would be reposing a phallus as big as the smile which he flashed at her as he beckoned her to the car. He was alone. She didn't ask why. The guilt wriggled up her neck but she pushed it back down again and crossed her legs.

They drove for about half-an-hour, heading west towards the hilly country where crags smashed down into the ocean and gentle orange groves sat amongst the grass. This country was like that - passion and gentleness all mixed together. The best of all worlds.

"I must thank you for... the other day. I'd have been totally lost."

He shook his head.

"It was nothing. You would have found your way. I think you're that sort of woman, no?"

He glanced over at her for a brief moment.

"What do you mean?"

"Strong and intelligent. And you do not look old enough to have a grown-up daughter."

"Bah!" she guffawed.

"Why do you put yourself down?"

"You don't know me."

There was an awkward silence, then she went on, "What about Rachel?"

He exhaled slowly, like a smoker.

"Rachel, Rachel..."

For a while, she thought he wasn't going to say anything.

Then all of a sudden he pulled the car over and stopped the engine.

"Rachel came here five years ago..."

"Seven," she said, then instantly regretted speaking.

"...She said, seven."

He looked her straight in the eye. Those hazelnut eyes of his.

"Five years ago. She was very unhappy. She was spending a lot of money, seeing a lot of men. Different men."

His voice dropped almost to a tremble. The ocean crashed over the rocks below Lucy's door. They were overlooking a narrow gorge. The light was fading fast but she thought his face had grown sad. He seemed older than his years.

"I took her in. I felt sorry for her. She is older than me. Maybe you noticed. And now she won't let go. She drinks... like a fish. Sometimes, she's fine – like the other day when you met her. But mostly, I have to do everything. She..."

He buried his head in his hands.

"...She brings other men home."

Lucy was stunned. She hadn't expected this. So she had been right about the smell of alcohol on Rachel's breath and about the crow's feet. The woman's face stretched before her, a mass of vice and fag-end smiles.

"Why...?" she began.

He looked round at her. She felt her heart melt when she gazed into his poor, soft eyes.

"Why don't you just... throw her out, or something?"

She couldn't believe she was saying this. And yet, it gave her a wriggling thrill to be speaking dangerously. To be evil.

The ocean swept its bulk out of the rising darkness and smashed itself on the rocks below.

"Because she's my wife."

He started the car.

When they reached the restaurant, neither spoke at first. Lucy felt shocked and angry. Why hadn't he told her? Now she was out on a date with a man ten – maybe fifteen – years younger than herself and he was married to the only person who had befriended her since her arrival. She wasn't sure whether it was anger, or guilt that made her speak. She slapped shut the menu.

"Why didn't you tell me?"

"Would you have still come with me?"

Melanie Desmoulins

"I don't know. Probably not."

"So."

"But that doesn't make it right."

He did not reply. Lucy felt the need to go on.

"But I can't just..."

"What? "

"I hardly know you."

"Do any of us really know anyone else?"

"You know Rachel."

His gaze fell.

"Do you still love her?"

"I felt sorry for her – at the start – and I thought I loved her. Now... I don't know."

He sighed. His eyes grew sad again.

"Can't we just enjoy this evening?" he pleaded, "I am sorry if I misled you. Please accept my apology."

She turned away.

"What would you like to eat?"

She could walk out now and that would be the end of it. She would spend the rest of her holiday in the way in which her daughter had intended her to spend it and then she would return to her home, her job, her life. She could walk out now but where would she go? Besides, the restaurant was in the middle of a small fishing-village. You needed a car to get there. She opened the menu again.

"I'll have the *Amejoas na cataplana*," she said clumsily.

"A good choice. It is a speciality of this region. I think I'll have the same."

"This was my daughter's idea, this holiday. I'm not sure if it was good one."

There was a pause as the waiter laid the table.

"You must have married very young."

She smiled.

"At eighteen. I did my training later. I'm a secretary."

"Ah, typewriters and ink."

She chuckled, wryly.

"Yes, it's pretty boring, I suppose, compared to what you do. But it has its moments."

She paused.

"...No, it doesn't."

They giggled. Suddenly he stopped.

He looked her straight in the eye. He kept doing that. It was most disconcerting.

"I'm not just a chef."

She felt her curiosity rise.

"The chef business is just a hobby, really. I sell my services to various restaurants, from time to time. Actually, I export almonds."

"Almonds," she repeated.

"Yes. It sounds kind of boring, too. But it's not. I was brought up on a farm. You get to watch the trees grow from seed to trunk, you get to see them stretch their arms and become branches, you get to see twigs being born and best of all, you're there when the spring bursts into blossom. That's next month."

His eyes had grown more and more intense while he's been speaking. The hazel in their centres had softened and begun to glow with the warmth of spring sunshine. She thought she remembered him saying that he owned the restaurants, but it didn't matter. In her mind, the truth grew and lengthened, till she felt it could be bent or twisted indefinitely, or might even curve itself into any form it wanted to.

"What do your family think of Rachel?"

His mood changed.

"Do we have to talk about her?"

"She is your wife."

"That was a mistake. A big mistake. When she first arrived, I don't know, I was attracted to her. She was older, more experienced. I kind of looked up to her. My mother died when I was only four years old. I don't remember her. Maybe it was something to do with that. She didn't have the drink problem, then. She seemed to be... not afraid of life."

"You said she was unhappy."

"There was that, too. We needed each other – then."

"Do you still love her?"

The hazel had hardened to young wood.

"No. Not for a long time. Our love perished in the winter of the mountains."

She wondered what he meant.

"Why am I telling you all this?"

"You asked *me* out – remember?"

He smiled and she returned the smile. She felt something slip inside of her. Ever so slightly. A part of her didn't like that, she'd kept herself from slipping, from ever giving of herself for so long. He belonged to another woman – no matter what she was, she was still his wife – and then, what would Jane have thought? What would her boss have thought? They seemed so far away here in the warm Algarve but one day soon, she would have to go back, would have to look them in the eye, would have to face herself in the dark of their eyes. Another part of her being, a tiny, fragile part, a part without words, desperately wanted to throw all caution to the winds, wanted more than anything to possess this man beneath the blossom of his almond grove, to wallow in the pleasures of the flesh...

"My family come from Alemtejo. They cut me off after Rachel came along. We did not marry in a church."

She was startled out of her reverie.

"So, what are you going to do. I mean, you are still a young man."

"Old in heart."

"Nonsense!"

"She has worn me down. Oh, she has money – so much money, she can afford to drink it all away and there will still be enough left over to drink some more."

"That's not why you married her..." Lucy immediately regretted having said this. He looked at her and his unhappy eyes tore at her very soul.

"You think that? You think that all Portuguese men are just looking for a rich bitch to come along and screw? Take them for their money?"

"No, no, I didn't mean..."

"What did you mean?"

"I meant the opposite. You had your own money from the almond groves and the chef's business. I mean you did, didn't you?"

He grabbed hold of her hand. She felt the smooth yet firm tan of his grip. A feeling of unhappiness – that, and something else...

"Listen. I have had to build what I've got with my own hands. I came here with very little – a little training in cuisine and a little money. That was all. It doesn't go very far – not even here, not even then. I worked hard, I invested wisely and now I have built up enough to be comfortable. That's all anyone can ask. With Rachel, I thought I had found happiness..."

He let go of her hand and threw his into the air in a gesture of hopelessness. She could still feel the sweat of his palm upon her knuckles, she could still feel the throb of his pulse along the tip of her index finger, the imprint of his golden ring in her skin. Slowly, she looked up at him.

"Why don't you get a divorce?"

She felt more evil than she had ever felt in her entire life. And it felt good.

"It's not so easy. Not in Portugal. Anyway, I don't know what she would do."

There was a pause. The restaurant was quiet tonight. Only two or three other couples were sitting at tables, and all were well out of earshot. The light caught his hand. The ring he was wearing swirled around his finger in the shape of a serpent. She had never seen one like it.

"I'm sorry," he said," You're supposed to be on holiday to get away from it all and here I am, giving you all my worries."

He paused again.

"You must know something."

She tried not to breathe too loudly. She thought the couple by the other wall would be able to hear her heartbeat as it pounded against her breast.

"Our meeting yesterday by the beach was not an accident. I recognised you as you climbed across the rocks, I watched you as you sat drinking, I wanted to have the courage to go up and talk to you then. The taxi problem gave me an excuse."

Before she could properly take this in, the sound of guitar strings startled both of them out of their conversation. On a slightly-raised dais, a musician was playing what looked like a lute, plucking and strumming while a heavy-breasted woman with jet-black hair done up in a bun cleared her throat into the microphone.

"They have *fado* every evening," Antonio informed her.

"...*Fado*? What's that?"

He began to explain but just then the singer let out an enormous caterwaul and the guitar followed suit. The sound which the strings made was not like a Spanish guitar but seemed to Lucy to resemble more that of a mandolin or banjo – not that she was any expert on musical instruments. She'd had a few piano lessons while at school but had soon given up. She wasn't musical, as her mother had said. You either had it or you didn't. And she didn't. The singing was by turns, plaintive and forceful, mournful and passionate. It swept up from the depths of the turquoise ocean and wrapped around her heart, it tore down from the peaks of high sierras like a herd of wild serpents in winter and fell upon her soul, without mercy, without guilt. She understood none of the words and yet she knew what the song was about for she too, had felt the ice touch of tragedy, she too had been through the loss of one loved more than herself, a love she had discovered too late. It was always too late. She was left chasing after herself like a snake after its tail. She never knew whether she was heading towards the beginning, or the end. She felt the tears spring to her eyes. She wanted it to stop, she needed desperately for it to go on and on and to never leave her. Never. She felt the touch of Antonio's hand. She spun round. Tears were rolling down her cheeks. His eyes were filled with sorrow and... something else. Rachel flashed through her mind but didn't seem to matter. Jane came and went in the flick of years. They had their own lives to lead. She didn't judge them, so why should they judge her? And Peter, Peter came into her eyes. Peter as a young man, Peter making love, Peter dying, Peter in his coffin... cold. She shuddered. Antonio squeezed her hand all the more tightly, as if he somehow knew what she was thinking, as if to say, he understood. Life had to go on, Peter wouldn't have wanted her in widow's weeds forever. But then, how the hell would she know what Peter would've wanted. He'd shot his seed into her, night after night (after a while, it had been once a month, actually) and yet she'd never really known him. Not really. And when she'd needed to, it was too late. It was always too late. Her hand was hurting. She pulled away. Then she looked into Antonio's eyes. Quickly, she reached out her hand again and grabbed his. He seemed surprised. She returned his grip, digging her long nails like those of Christ's executioner into his palm. He winced, but not with pain. Everybody was clapping around them. The music had stopped. The couple by the window were framed in gold against the black of night, held in an embrace tighter than the tautest strings ever plucked.

In the room upstairs, there were bars on the head-board of the bed. Lucy's fingers were white with the pressure of gripping onto these brass struts. Antonio wanted her from behind most of the time, and she let him have his way. Sometimes he would be in her anus, sometimes in her vagina. The sensation was different, one from the other. In the vagina, it was like a ramrod, hot and bulging. In the shit-hole, he became a sword, slicing with white-hot pain. And yet, she found that she liked it, both ways. She liked the curve of butt upon butt, the angle of thigh upon angle of thigh. She enjoyed being as a beast. He massaged her as he spoked her butt, and she came five times that night. He spunked into her body three times, but then she took him in the mouth and made him erupt twice more. His great, swollen member almost choked her, but she would gladly have died in the midst of the ecstasy which he was giving her.

Gladly.

four

The mastic tree is a tree with many branches, the fruit of which are little red berries, which grow black when they ripen. If you wish to acquire strength for coitus, take the fruit, pound them and macerate them with oil and honey; then drink of the liquid first thing in the morning: you will thus become vigorous for the coitus.

Lucy went down to the beach. She spread her enormous floral towel and laid herself down, legs together, her body facing upwards in the light of the already rampant morning sun. Bit by bit, she gently rubbed the Factor 8 into her still pale skin. She had decided to get a tan, after all. Her limbs seemed to have grown years younger since last night. Her hair glowed with a fire she had never thought imaginable. She could feel her cheeks fill with her heart's blood and her knees soften like those of a young girl. She let her eyes close slowly, shutting out the sun bit by bit like doors retreating from a furnace. She had drunk quite a lot last night – for her, at any rate – the *vinho verde* had been delicious and Antonio... Antonio was charming, sensual, manly, kind... she ran out of epithets. He was everything you could look for in a man. Her mind drifted upon the wave...

Once, there was a rock. And the rock was dead. It saw nothing, it sensed nothing. Cold winds would rake across its body, hard rain smash down from the sky, and still it would know nothing. Far beneath the rock, there lay an underground lake. The lake had no face. It was like an empty mirror. Beside the water, in the deepest dark imaginable, there slept a snake. Suddenly the snake awoke. A yellow eye saw the lake and the serpent went to drink of the cool water. Because the lake had never been partaken of before, the sensuous body of the snake caused the mirror to break and ripple with delight and from its faceless face, there grew a tree. The tree stretched upwards in the dank dark until at last it came to rest beneath the dead boulder. Because the tree had given the lake a face at last, the face smiled upon the boulder's belly and a breeze – the first ever – snaked upwards and caused the rock to split into two. Through the crack the tree swelled, until the gap had grown large enough to allow the stiff rod of its trunk to force its way through the dead stone. And as it stretched amongst the tiny particles of rock and dirt, the tree's rough bark awoke each minuscule piece of grit, so that the stone parted without meaning to. One day, when the sky was at rest and streams flowed like blood into the sea, the tree at last burst up and pierced through the thick integument of stone and took its first breath of air.

Suddenly he was there, beside her. He began to stroke her arms and legs, causing invisible hairs to rise, to greet the warm palms of his hands. His long body arched down by hers. They touched, the softest of tingling touches. Rivulets coursed through her, opening her up and spreading her out. A pain began inside her. The rivulets joined and became a river and the pain grew intense. Unbearable. No words slipped from his mouth, only the heat of his breath, warmer even than the sun's own, burning through her mouth, filling up her lungs with the most exquisite of tortures. Her back arched involuntarily as he ran his fingers over her tautened nipples, raising them to a pitch of frenzy so that the stars around them pressed shamelessly against her blue bikini. She didn't care who might be watching them, for her eyes had glazed over and no-one else existed on the beach. Nobody lived in the world except Antonio. She tried to whisper his name but had no breath left in her chest. His lips were upon hers in a pressed kiss. He moved his hand down over her midriff, her thighs, her knees which ran like water, her delicate feet with their newly-painted nails. Shivers slid up and down her spine like tiny silverfish. She was his whore. Yes! She was his concubine, his slave-girl, his piece of flesh. And yet, she was the mistress of his soul. The ruler of his cock. The lady of his seed. Now it was her turn. She was on the brink. The pain had reached a level which was beyond endurance. She wanted to have him, to wrestle him into the sand and force his manhood into her softening body, to feel the lips of the star tickle at her back, tear at her buttocks, scorch the soles of her feet. She bit his lower lip, pulling him towards her. She felt his sweat upon her cheeks, she felt the hot breath of his silent desire burn her closed eyelids, she felt him mount her and press the swollen member of his masculinity against her moistening thighs...

Something fell across her face and rolled down her cheek. She blinked and opened her eyes. A brightly-coloured ball lay beside her face. A small child ran up and jumped over her. Sand flew into her face. She coughed and spluttered and propped herself up on her elbows. She had sand in her mouth. As she brushed it off her bikini, she was embarrassed to find her nipples hard as hazelnuts. Flecks of sand had stuck to the perspiration on her skin, forming neat little brown beads all over her chest. Then she realised with a thump what had happened. It had never happened to her before. She had never allowed it to. She glanced around as she felt the colour rise to her cheeks. The beach was peppered with a smattering of people. Lucy felt as though everyone had watched her as she slept, as her shame had revealed itself to the open sky, to the cold ocean... she shivered and drew her arms around her body. What was she thinking? How could she? A woman of her years. It was pathetic. This man was another woman's husband. He was ten years younger than her. She was supposed to be on holiday for a rest, not to engage in the pleasures of the flesh. It had to be the sun. That was it. The Portuguese sun had gone to her head, causing a kind of madness. She crossed one leg over the other and dared not look down. After a while, she got up and walked gingerly towards the sea. She waded in. It was chilly. She liked that. She died for an instant as she plunged into the waters. She needed to immerse herself in the freezing frigidity of the Atlantic, needed to feel its deathly undertow pull her tarted toes into line, let it enter into her body and wash away the filth of her sex.

When she returned to the hotel, Rachel was there.

"Hi, darling. Had a good day?"

Lucy was taken off-guard. She felt her voice tremble upon the brink she thought she had just conquered. She cracked a smile onto her face.

"Almost got a tan!"

She tried to sound bright as a blustery Spring day, as if nothing had happened. Perhaps, nothing had. But it was a lie.

"It's taken me years to get a tan. A real tan, that is. One which stays, no matter what. You're blonde and you've managed to get one in a day! There's no justice."

Lucy wondered if there had been a cynical edge to Rachel's comment but then she dismissed the thought. How could she know anything? She had on a thin, black dress which reached almost to her toes and yet seemed to reveal everything. It was then Lucy noticed the man standing behind Rachel. He was thin, short and deathly pale and was clad in white suit which, in the blazing noonday sun made him seem a little like an apparition. He wore narrow, impenetrable sunglasses and had on a Panama hat. His shoes, like the rest of him, were gleaming bleached as the sides of a yacht and his hair was a peculiar shade of rabbit-white. He seemed twitchy, as if he were uncomfortable out there in the sun, as if he ought to have been shut away in a dark room, somewhere deep in the cellars of Albernoa. He seemed totally out of place here. Rachel introduced him.

"Bartolomeo, meet Lucy. Lucy – Bartolomeo. He's a good friend of mine."

Edging towards her, he did not offer his hand but merely nodded, slowly. His skin really was totally devoid of colour. Rachel suddenly seemed to have forgotten she was there. She did that a lot. It was quite irritating. She was speaking to the pale man in an almost confidential tone. Lucy was unable to make out what was being said. It may even have been in Portuguese. He shook his head and then Rachel seemed to become annoyed. The man glanced around nervously as Rachel put out her hand as if she were demanding something of him. They formed an odd couple there, on the hotel terrace – one in black, the other in white – almost like puppets moving on levers and strings. Somewhat reluctantly, Lucy thought – though it was hard to tell what was going on behind that white-suited face – he reached into his jacket and produced a package wrapped in paper. Even the paper was white. Rachel almost grabbed it from him. He turned on his heel and departed. His shoes made an odd, clicking sound as he left. Rachel smiled and pocketed the parcel. As if suddenly remembering Lucy's presence, she spun round.

"...He's an albino, you know."

"What?"

"An albino. He has no pigment in his skin, no melanin, so

he has to protect himself from the sun. Coming out like this is dangerous for him. He has to wear Factor 30 all the time!"

She laughed, and Lucy felt that she had no pity left in her soul.

"Imagine that! Being Portuguese and albino. A blond bombshell. What sodding rotten luck!"

"Poor man."

Rachel waved away her sympathy.

"He's a nothing. Worse than a nothing. You have to learn how to deal with these people."

Lucy found herself wondering how Antonio could ever have become embroiled with this woman. Perhaps it was for her money. But then, why would he be attracted to her, Lucy if all he were interested in was money? After all, he had many times her means. She was only a secretary, for God's sake.

"Come on, let's go for a drink," Rachel urged.

"I... I'd rather not."

"Oh come on, don't be a spoil-sport. Just one."

"No, no, really, I've had too much sun already. If I take a drink, I'll be sick. You go on, though."

Rachel sighed.

"Oh well, alone again..."

She turned away and trotted towards the bar. Her walk was not quite straight. Her buttocks swung from side to side as though they were trying to entice the air.

δδδδδδδδδδδδ

It was early evening. Lucy and Antonio were seated at a café. This time, she had not needed an invitation. Antonio looked down.

"What do you do, when someone you once loved falls apart before your eyes, becomes repulsive, arrogant, hateful...? What do you do, when you know that you don't love her any more?"

She paused.

"I think you must face it. Face the truth."

"The truth. The hardest thing in the world."

"Does she still love you?"

He sighed.

"Ah... who knows? Who knows what goes on in that wine-soaked brain?"

There was an awkward silence, but though Lucy shifted in her seat, she felt strangely comfortable. It were as if she was putting on an awkwardness, simply because she felt afraid of the comfort which she felt in this man's presence. She was getting used to acting again.

"Antonio... can I ask you something?"

He looked up. She went on.

"Where do I fit into all of this?"

A smile broke out across his face, teasing the corners of his eyes in the dying sunlight. He reached across the white tablecloth and touched her hand. His fingers were strong and masculine, warm with the blood of the sun.

"I've never felt so happy as when I'm with you. You take all my worries away. I have enjoyed these few days more than any I can remember."

He paused and let his gaze fall. Then he looked at her.

"I think I'm falling in love with you."

She felt herself blush. Now it was her turn to look down. A gentle breeze wafted the corners of the white cotton. She felt like a schoolgirl, out on her first date. A pimply girl, all stutters and stammers and tripping over feet. Not like Antonio. She smiled. His hand was still upon hers. It felt good. She looked up again.

"Antonio..." she began, but it was too late, for he had already moved around the table and his eyes now gazed into hers. They were only inches apart. She could feel his hot breath pour upon her lips. She closed her eyes and felt her mouth moisten.

"Lucy," he groaned as he slipped his arm around her waist. She felt the fingers tighten, the long firm fingers of his hand. With his other hand, he tilted her chin upwards. She felt the soft warmth of his full lips push gently between hers like twin palms of love. She tasted the coffee of his passion. His tongue teased at her teeth, prodding and then withdrawing, and with each withdrawal she longed ever more for its return. She pressed her lips harder against him, urging him to come back to her. And he did, and their tongues wound deliciously around one another in the hotbed of her mouth, tickling her gums, the sides of her cheeks, her palate so exquisite, so delightful, so wondrous... At last, their lips parted. Both were panting. Lucy realised she had hardly had time to breathe amidst the passion of his embrace. She felt shame wash from her ears, outward. This was too much. She couldn't. She got up, inadvertently knocking over her glass. The winestain spread like blood over the cloth.

"I'm sorry... I can't do this. Sorry."

She walked away.

"Wait! Lucy – wait."

His voice was insistent but it grew more faint as she moved across the terrace. She did not look back. Once outside the café, she broke into a run.

When Lucy awoke the next morning, she was still in her evening clothes. They were creased like a sorry party. She was stiff. It was already hot. She felt suddenly sticky and tore them off as she dived into the shower. The cool water ran down over her hair, shoulders, breasts and back, soothing her shame, returning her to an innocence of a kind. And with the innocence, came guilt. A woman her age shouldn't be running about getting involved with these people. She knew nothing about them. She had been bewitched by the sun and the wine and... Antonio.

As she emerged from the bathroom drying her hair, she noticed a small, white envelope had been slipped beneath the door. She wasn't sure whether it had been there when she awoke, or whether someone had pushed it under while she'd been in the shower. She knelt down and picked it up. She turned it over in her hands. The envelope was blank. Shouldn't she just toss it away? That was the right thing to do, the sensible thing. End it there. But then, perhaps it wasn't from him, at all. Who else could it be, but him? Without really knowing why, she ripped it open. The note read:

Lucy. My dear Lucy. I must see you again. 19.30, by the disused fishermen's wharf. Please do not walk away this time. I love you.

—*Antonio*

An electric eel coursed through her belly and up her spine.

She folded it shut.

Something told her to throw it away. To finish it. It was the command of her mother, long ago. It was the urging of her daughter, not yet born. It was her own life's order. And yet in the depths beyond herself, a wordless voice whispered to her, for once to be led by her instincts rather than the dusty keys of logic and reason for once, in sunlight and blood to abandon the steel and porcelain of the widow and to run naked with the wind.

She placed the note on the dresser and went back into the bathroom.

She gazed at herself in the full-length mirror. She ran the tips of her fingers down over her temples, cheeks, jawline, neck, breasts, waist and thighs. She was still young, her skin was still taut and creamy as buttermilk, her hair was still soft and long and golden. She had a lot to give, and a right to take from life that which she desired. Life was too short for guilt and too long for misery. She had realised that too late with Peter. Poor Peter. The words had gone together in her mind for so long that she had become unable to prise them apart. And perhaps there was reason for that. She sighed. Then she looked herself straight in the eye. Perhaps for the first time in her life. She smiled and the face in the mirror smiled back. Antonio had a right to happiness, to a life away from that drunken tart he was with. So did she. It had to be good. She felt her shame slip away as the towel fell from her shoulders.

Deep in the oldest part of the old town, the whore was drifting. Her painted face relaxed as it never did while she was awake, and she fled into the fields of purity. For no-one is evil while they sleep. The men she'd serviced were laid in cuts upon the walls all around her and the sun shone in the dark, illuminating each one of them in turn. A line stretching back twenty years, to the time when her virgin cunt had been sliced in two by the very first invading prick. She had been only thirteen. Just born. Born to be a whore. It was a job, like any other. Neither good, nor evil. She'd long since stopped asking herself whether what she was doing was right or wrong. Only in her sleep did the old demons, the kindly old demons of the Lord return to fret her with their silly smiles and stern warnings. The sins of the flesh were hers and wasn't Our Lord's fancy-woman, a whore, after all? And now she's a saint. So there was still hope. The whore's mouth opened slightly, to reveal a row of blackened teeth and the sweet smell of tired lust. In a hundred years, she would be dead. The daylight was her bed, and she was everyone else's. In a funny way, she was God. She laughed in her open-mouthed sleep. The laugh fled around the room in the shape of a serpent and slunk out through the crack in the window-sill.

It was dusk when she went down to the old wharf. They

said the Moors used to fish off here and after the men of the south had been driven out by the Catholic Kings, the bay had become a haven for smugglers and their whores. Ordinary fishermen forged life and stone from the sea and the sea gave of itself, both life and death as the centuries sailed on. But the wind of the south had faded and now the wharf was no longer used. It jutted out into the darkness of the ocean as if it hankered only for the past. A chilly breeze had drifted through the town earlier in the evening but this had fallen so that the unusual warmth for the time of year continued. As she descended the steps, she made out his form, standing upon the wooden wharf. He was gazing out to sea and didn't notice her arrival at first. As she stepped onto the boards, he spun round. He came towards her but then stopped. Then more slowly, they moved together. He placed his hands upon her shoulders and gently pulled her to him. She felt her resistance fall away just as the cold breeze had vanished from the air.

"Oh Lucy, I'm glad you are here. I was afraid you wouldn't come."

"I'm glad, too," she said as their lips met. Their kisses were soft, tender, tentative at first as if they had just met after a long separation but they grew more passionate as he squeezed her body against his. She clasped his broad shoulders, she felt soft and warm as she sank into his strong grip, she felt the tickle of his fingertips as they played up and down her back, the male scent of his wavy, black hair as she nestled her nose into the space between his shoulder and his ear. It wasn't aftershave, it was the scent of passion. The oldest perfume of all. He was wearing a dark cotton suit with an open-necked shirt. She had on a navy-blue summer skirt and matching blouse. She could feel the very patterns of his fingerprints as they teased her skin. He ran his hands down over her shoulders, the pit of her back, her buttocks, her arms, her breasts. She arched backwards. The stars shone bright in the clear winter light. She felt the force of his male desire and she felt herself grow warm and wet between her legs. Her thighs parted. An image of the couple huddled in the doorway in the rain and the night flashed through her mind. She smiled as she kissed him. She was the ungainly doll, she was the shadow of lust upon the wall. The woman in the alleyway was close by her. Her invisible back ran with the curve of her own spine in the growing darkness, the swelling of her breasts grew to a point with her own nipples, her eyelids closed over the same gleaming stars. She could hear him panting in the night and was aware of her own rasping breaths, hot as the moon's face. He led her over to a small, sheltered cove and they sat down on the sand. It was still warm. He lay back, his hands behind his head. She lay beside him and both of them gazed at the stars and the moon and the black sky. She was perfectly happy and could've stayed there forever. Never mind, that dawn would come and wipe the stars like tears from the face of the sky. Never mind, that people would cast glances upon them. Never mind, that here was she, mother and widow having an affair (the word made her shiver inside) with a foreigner. She didn't care what anyone thought or saw. She wanted to shout it out loud, to run without halter or saddle across the golden sand and the newly-greened grass and scream, I'm in love! I'm in love!!! and let the sad world hear her and let it burn in its envy, for all she cared. She felt her heart beat faster and harder as if it wanted to rise up out of her breast and be free at last. She could hear him in the darkness, breathing beside her. She turned over onto her side and leaned on her elbow. She ran her finger down over his forehead, nose, lips, chin then down onto his chest, midriff and down each thigh in turn. Through the cotton, he seemed to stiffen. Deliberately slowly, she undid the buttons of his shirt, one by one. She tossed aside the flaps. More vigorously now, she ran all the fingers of one hand over his hairless chest and down over his stomach and haunches. He groaned gently. She liked that. She liked him opening up, becoming vulnerable. She tickled around his nipples and then leaned over him and kissed him softly upon the lips. He met her kiss and their touch lasted for a delicious eternity. Something seemed to snap inside him, as if he had deliberately been holding back, been restraining himself in order that the eventual moment be all the more pleasurable. He grabbed her and rolled her over onto her back. She could feel the sweat of his palms upon her spine. Feverishly, he tore off her clothes. First to go was her low-cut dress. He kissed her all over and moaned,

"I love you, Lucy my darling, my moon, my stars, my everything. I love you."

He undid her bra and slid it off with ease. He tossed it onto the sand like a conquest. She slid her fingers beneath the belt of his trousers and eased them off, running her nails along the backs of his

Melanie Desmoulins

thighs as she did so. He kissed her breasts, sucking at them, drawing their already erect nipples into ever firmer erection. He ran his tongue down the sides of her breasts, making her want to scream like a lunatic with the delicious torture of his tongue-tip.

"Give me your wet cunt," he whispered.

In a moment, they were utterly naked and he pressed his body close to hers. His mule passion was swollen and hardened. He ran it over her face, her breasts, her navel, her thighs, her feet, tickling her gently and yet with a delicious urgency. It was like another tongue.

"No more," she moaned, closing her eyes, "No more."

But he was relentless. He rolled her over onto her front. She felt the warm sand rise to meet her breasts, her thighs, the backs of her arms, she felt it surge up between her legs where she had grown warm and wet. He kissed her all over her back, her buttocks, the insides of her knees. He urged her legs apart and ran his demon-sized cock along her wet lips, stroking up and down, up and down. She arched back and threw him off. She felt herself stiffen between her lips. She wanted him. On all fours, he ran at her and bit her on the shoulder. She rolled over onto her back and whispered, "Now, Antonio, now. Please, please, please."

Mounting her, he forced her legs apart. She resisted, knowing that the more she fought, the sweeter would be the conquest for both of them. Bending his head down to her mound of Venus, he thrust his tongue deep into her, pulling out and in, out and in, out and in with his burning breath upon her clit, his panting in tune with the rise and fall of her belly. She dug her nails into the sand and then into the skin of his shoulder. Her feet slapped up onto the sides of his buttocks. She wanted to crush him forever. Just before she came, he pulled out his tongue, turned her over and rammed his thick rod into her. His manhood filled her up until she felt she would burst. He began thrusting, slowly at first and then faster and faster until the hot blood flowed from beneath her fingers into the dark sand and she felt the great warmth of the earth below rise and fill her body. Her head buzzed and she roared with triumph. Just then, his back, his beautiful, curved back arched and he thrust his feet rearward into the hot sand. His maleness writhing within her swelled magnificently as it reached for her heart. She felt the throb of his climax. She felt the warm wetness of his release. He remained taut for a long moment and then eased down onto her back.

"You're wonderful, you're God." he gasped.

Her eyes still closed, she smiled ever so slightly. She was still coming.

That night, no faecal demons were released upon the coast.

Melanie Desmoulins

five

A remedy for a man with a small member, who wants to make it grand or fortify it for the coitus, consists in a compound made of a moderate quantity of pepper, lavender, galanga and musk, reduced to a powder, sifted, and mixed up with honey and preserved ginger. The member, after having been first washed in warm water, is then vigorously rubbed with the mixture; it will then grow large and brawny, and afford to the woman a marvellous feeling of voluptuousness.

Up in the high mountains that were beyond the horizon's horizon, a man lay nailed to a boulder. He was totally naked and the blood dripped in thick gouts from the smashed palms which had once played symphonies, painted masterpieces, penned classics. He was standing upright and all down his sides were scored the marks of a severe beating. He was bearded but the hair had been torn off in places, burned off in others. A large "S" covered his chest and there were dark burns on his genitals. Before him lay a pitcher of water but he was unable to reach it. The water had once been filled with ice but now the day's heat had melted the ice and with it had gone the man's eternal soul. His head hung over his chest. He was unconscious. Around his lips drooled the cunt-juice of the whore. He had come here, to this rock, because she had willed it. She had desired it. His cock had followed her command. His cock which was still erect. Still stiff as a pole. He had given everything to her. He had given her his all. But it was not enough. It would never be good enough. She was insatiable. Like a serpent, she had no end. Suddenly he awoke and screamed. The scream travelled in a circle all over the deep valley, up into the empty sky, out across the invisible sea which lay beyond the horizon's horizon. His head slumped down again. A stream of saliva, thick and glaucous like semen, issued from the corner of his mouth and was caught in the sun's rays. The silver stream glistened in the wondrous light. A bird circled overhead, noiselessly. His last breath, though never far away, seemed an eternity in coming. The long trail to decomposition had already begun when at last, with an animal groan, his cock discharged its foul, joyous packet of gout, and with that, he perished. His eyes were the first to die.

δδδδδδδδδδδδ

Lucy and Rachel were sitting at a beachside bar, sipping from glasses of sangria. Rachel stroked her fine, golden hair, sifting it like ripe corn through her long, whore's fingers.

"You're beginning to look like a blonde bombshell."

She paused.

"You *are* a blonde bombshell."

"I've never been called that, before."

"You're joking."

"No. Never. It doesn't seem right, somehow..."

Lucy smiled.

"...but I like being one."

Rachel's brow furrowed.

"What is right, and what is wrong? I never know why people stick these labels onto things. Things are things, nothing more, nothing less. They just are. You either take advantage of them or else are taken advantage of. You're either a winner or a loser. That's all there is to it."

The sangria was stronger than she had reckoned. It always hit you later. Before Lucy knew what she was saying, it was out.

"...Like you took advantage of Antonio?"

Rachel was silent for a moment. She seemed stunned.

"What are you talking about?"

Her tone of voice said to Lucy, *You have ventured too far across the invisible boundary which lies between holiday acquaintances destined never to meet again. You have no right. You should feel ashamed of yourself for your gaucheness. Don't think for one minute that just because I seem to be nice to you, it means that you can somehow suddenly become part of my family, my world, me.*

Rachel did not say all of this. She did not need to. Instead, she went on, "I had more money than him. Oh..." she tossed her hand into the air, "He had his moments but now, I find he has become boring. Afraid. I didn't come here for that."

"What did you come here for?"

"What's this with all the questions? What business is it of yours?"

She paused, as if half-expecting an answer, or even an apology but when none was forthcoming, she seemed unable to stop.

"I don't know, really. The sun, I suppose. That's a big part of it. The sun, and everything that goes with it. I wanted to get away from losers, to get some sex and enjoy life a bit – and what's wrong with that?"

She tilted her chin up as if daring Lucy to riposte. She had a chiselled chin, as though some Michelangelo of the wine-bar had moved in one night and given her a perfect countenance.

"But everything gets boring after a while, don't you think? Even sex."

"Is that why you drink so much... is that why you do drugs?"

Lucy was astounded at her own courage. The sangria must have been strong.

"...Perhaps."

Now Lucy was the one who couldn't stop.

"Who is the man in the white suit?"

Rachel looked puzzled for a moment.

"Oh – him. Don't ask. Just don't ask."

She paused.

"Listen, dear. There are things that go on here that you wouldn't believe, I mean you simply wouldn't believe."

"Like what?"

Rachel pondered for a moment. She was clearly the worse for drink. That's what happened to people who had drunk too much, for too many years. It ended up so they simply couldn't take it any more. One glass, and they'd be swill-eyed. Carefully, she opened up a cigarette packet, lit a fag and took one long draw.

"Like the boats from Africa. Big long boats. They bring in

this, that... and the next thing."

She giggled obscenely. Lucy wished she would put out her cigarette. It wasn't that Lucy was a teetotaller type when it came to fags – far from it, she had smoked a pretty packet or two, in her day. But she'd given up five years ago. Just stopped, one crisp winter's day. The type of day that blew your lungs out with the joy of life. Hadn't started again, even after Peter died. But Rachel's whole manner was beginning to rile. Her supercilious demeanour, her sleaze, her lack of right and wrong... but then, what Lucy had done wasn't exactly goody two-shoes, either. But at least, she knew it was wrong – or at least, not wholly right. All was fair in...

For the first time in two years, she found herself needing a fag. And the funny thing was, she didn't know why. She felt herself giggle and then hated herself for doing it. Damn sangria. Went to your head without you realizing. Rachel thought she was laughing with her, and leaned closer.

"...Want to try some, dear?"

Lucy was startled but tried not to show it.

"No... No, thanks. I'll stick with this." she said, pointing to the sangria.

Rachel slapped her hand down on the table.

"Boring. I thought so."

"What do the long boats bring in?"

"The long boats bring in miracles and joy."

"What do you mean?"

"Look, darling. They bring in whatever you want. If it's drugs, they've got that. If it's long, muscular thighs, bulging balls and streaming cocks, they've got that, too. Understand?"

She swayed a little as she got up.

"Well, I'm off. See you later. Maybe."

She tottered out, leaving a trail of mixed drinks and stale cigarettes. She was totally repulsive. But Lucy found herself unable to dislike.

Lucy was never sure whether Rachel had been offering her a fag or some strange drug, or the smooth, blue-veined cock of a young African. Despite herself, she found that she desired Rachel's body. She wanted to feel the smooth contours of her animal skin, she wanted to flick her tongue over the fruits of her sex. Her breasts would be as ripe melons beneath her experienced fingers. She let her head fall back, let her closed eyes absorb the golden sun. The juices of sex oozed out from every pore in her lithe body. Each sweat gland spasmed in an orgasm of its own. From the prickling spew-cysts of her vulva, there leaked the slimy residue of female desire, a demon for each gushing gland, a tiny satan with each fevered outpouring. Her long legs stretched out. Men had once died for those legs, she thought. Before Peter. And now, they would die again. She would be the satanic altar-vulva, she would be the anus of Persephone in Hell's endless throat, she, Lucy-the-secretary with her long legs, would become the icon of a million masturbating schoolboys. Rachel had long legs, too. She and the dark-haired cat were twins. Sexual twins. In her mind they were lithe, perfectly-merging in the way only two women can. In her mind they were making love, long and slow in the hot afternoon. Blonde upon raven-haired. Cunt upon cunt. Female juices lingered and swam around the lips of their swollen love-mouths. They yelled in unison like dogs, like bitches-on-heat. Their vulvas gaped, yelling shamelessly. Twin whores. Blood sisters. Sex twins. They drew one another's body into themselves, into the red heat of their fuck-holes. They licked at one another's butts, creaming around the crumpled skin of the anus. Lucy drew her head back out of the dream. She wondered what she would do when she found out about Antonio and her. Would she care? Or would she surprise her and lash out? She had creepy friends. The white-suited albino was a drug dealer, Lucy was sure. Then an awful thought struck her. What if Antonio were involved in some way? What if he was lying to her about the way he had acquired his money. What if he were lying to her about everything? What would she do? Oh don't be a stupid bitch, she thought. Why should he be involved – just because his drunken slut of a wife dallied with every vice in town and out, it didn't mean that he did. The wetness between her thighs was not just sweat.

As if to drown her thoughts, she took a large swig from the brightly-coloured liquid and let her face bask in the searing sunlight. She found herself able to hate. And the hate was the hate of love.

δδδδδδδδδδδδ

The man in the white suit hovered somewhere behind her as she sat on the hotel terrace. She could feel his eyes slide like a lizard's over her body and even from a distance, she was able to feel the touch of his dank, bloodless hands upon the small of her back. She shivered in the heat. He sidled up to her and without a word, sat down. He was sideways-on to her. She could make out his nose the shape of a saddle, his thin, inhuman lips, his pallid cheeks dry like the face of death. He wore thin, mirror sunglasses which reflected the terrace and the sky in a kind of bowl-shaped reverse of normal. He began to speak in a gluey voice and no-one except Lucy would have been able to hear what he was saying.

"How are you, Misses Thomas?"

"Very well, thank you," she replied, deliberately curt.

"Good, good." He seemed not to have noticed the inflection in her voice or if he had, then he was hiding it. He brought the tips of his fingers together as if he were pondering deeply upon something.

"You know," he began, "many tourists come here in these times. Many men and women and little children..."

His voice reminded her of a lizard, ducking and diving beneath the tables and never quite emerging into the light.

"Before the visitors came, this place was poor. Very poor. The people, they catch a few fish, they make a little cork..."

He threw his pale hands up in a gesture of hopelessness.

"...and now, look at this."

Lucy wondered what he was driving at. He had an odd turn of phrase. She couldn't quite figure it out. Archaic, almost. As though he had learned his English a very long time ago.

"I'm sorry, I don't think I caught your name."

She suddenly felt very English. There was nothing like imposing a bit of etiquette on a foreigner for that. It usually worked. Got them on the wrong foot. Made them all defensive. But he seemed not to have heard her and yet she knew that he had. He turned to look at her.

"Yes, you know my name. We met a few days ago. Have you forgotten?"

She felt herself fumbling. She had forgotten.

"Why are you here, Misses Thomas?"

She was disarmed.

"I... I'm on holiday."

"Ah yes, you are on holiday."

　　　　　　　　　　　　　Melanie Desmoulins

He looked away again. A silence grew in the space between them and filled up the entire terrace.

"*Senor* Antonio – he is nice?"

Lucy felt her anger rise.

"Listen. I don't know who are and what you're getting at..."

"We all have our ways. We, and the beasts which surround us. *Senor* Antonio has his, you have yours, I have mine. I do not interfere."

"...Interfere?"

"You are not a fool, I think."

Lucy couldn't believe she was having this conversation. She thought for a moment.

"Rachel. Is she involved in this?"

A smile almost broke out on his face. Almost.

"Rachel is sad and happy. *Senor* Antonio does not make her happy. What is wrong with a little *vinho*?"

"And drugs?"

"Ah... drugs, drugs, drugs."

He wheeled round again and looked her in the eye. She could see nothing behind the dark glass.

"Do not be the judge, lest you be judged."

He got up like a broken puppet. He touched his Panama hat. He was wearing a serpent ring.

"Good-day, Lucy."

As she watched him go, she wondered how he had known her first name. The terrace with its flat whitewash and its surly waiters seemed suddenly alien. She longed to be back home. Back in the safe non-entity which was neither evil, nor good. She felt a hand on her shoulder.

"Did I frighten you?"

It was Antonio. He kissed her and sat down. Embarrassed, she glanced around.

"You shouldn't do that here – what if Rachel were watching?"

"Why should she? Anyway – who cares if she is?"

He sat down beside her.

"Antonio, can I ask you something?"

He touched her hand gently.

"Of course, my love. Anything."

"You haven't heard the question yet."

He smiled, but the smile was a little strained, she thought.

"Who is the white-faced man?"

"Who?... Oh, you mean Bartolomeo. How did you meet him?"

"I didn't. He met me. He came and sat right where you're sitting, just five minutes ago."

Saying this, she glanced at her watch to find that almost half-an-hour had passed. She must've been dreaming of home for longer than she had thought.

"But I've seen him before. He was with Rachel. I had forgotten that. I don't know how I could have forgotten it."

"Oh...?"

He seemed amused. She felt angry.

"He supplies her with drugs... among other things."

"You know? But, I mean..."

"Rachel cannot exist in the real world. Perhaps she never has. Our marriage – for me, it was real. For her... who knows? Some people are like that. I'm not, but some people are."

"But how could you..." She was lost for words. This all seemed like a play. Her sense of alienness had grown and opened up into a wide, airless abyss. He sat back in his chair.

"Lucy. You are from a different country, a country where everything is black and white. Everything has a reason. I know – I lived there for three years. Remember?"

"You never told me that."

"Yes, I did. You've forgotten."

"I seem to be forgetting too much. You sound just like him."

"Who?"

"Him – the albino, or whatever he is."

He ignored her comment and went on.

"People like Rachel never fit in there, so they end up taking to drink or drugs, or something else. Her, it is different. It is a tourist trap. Right and wrong are relative terms, as much to do with the intention as the action. It is hard to be rigorous in a hot climate. Do you follow me?"

Lucy had removed her sunglasses and was staring at him. His English seemed suddenly to have improved.

"...What?" he asked, a little irritated.

"And what is your view, Antonio?"

"There you go again, always looking for right and wrong, innocent and guilty, good and evil. Why do you have to judge people?"

"Funny," she said.

"What is?"

"That's just what he said."

"Who?"

"Bartolomeo. He said 'who was I to judge him'."

He was silent. His breath fell.

"Perhaps I really don't belong here."

She got up and walked away.

"Wait!" he shouted, "Please wait."

But she had made up her mind. Whatever Antonio and his crazy compatriots were involved in, whatever good or evil or something-in-between, whatever space Rachel fitted into or didn't fit into, Lucy wanted no part of it. She had come here to relax and forget about it all, to forget her grief if that were possible and she really didn't need all this. She had her job and her family and that was all she needed. She was too old for romantic entanglements. She did not look back as she walked away. He ran up and grabbed her by the arm. She spun round. The snake ring around his finger grinned at her with its golden smile.

"Get away from me!" she screamed.

He let go as if he'd been bitten. People were looking at them.

"Don't come back," she hissed.

His glance fell.

She turned and stalked up to her room. He did not follow.

ᚖᚖᚖᚖᚖᚖᚖᚖᚖᚖᚖᚖᚖ

That night, Lucy masturbated for only the second time since Peter's death.

In her fantasy, she had two lovers. One, Bartolomeo, at her vagina, the other, a faecal demon, in her rectum. The demon had pink eyes.

When she awoke the next morning, she found that she had shitted into the sheets. The shit was white and solid. As she washed it down into the toilet-bowl, she found herself wishing instead that she had stuffed it into her mouth, had filled herself, like some demented Egyptian mummy, with the filthy dung from all the beasts she could lay her hands on. Yes! And in that waste, would she find that which she was. Lucy recoiled from the thought as she found herself becoming insanely aroused once again.

Melanie Desmoulins

six

The virile member, rubbed with asses milk, will become uncommonly strong and vigorous.

Night

The two pale-bodied women shine in the faint starlight, so they cover themselves with their own filth, and crouch naked behind the great rock. Waiting.

The olive-skinned youth wandered gingerly into the cove. He was almost blind in the dark. Just the curly-headed waves on his left and the gaunt boulder to his right.

He hears something

Stops

Moves on, uncertain now in his passion

He too, is entirely nude. Even the promises of wondrous delight, spun in his ear by the world-wise women, have failed to stiffen his penis.

He trips over a thick branch and falls headlong into the darkness.

The long-haired women spring on him

He shouts, once

Each mouth is filled with a vein, jugular

They bite. Together

The mouths fill with blood

The body twitches a few times, then grows limp

All except the phallus.

Blood still spurting across their shit-scrubbed cheeks, the women move down the thin corpse and begin to suck the tumid worm. The veins along its sides are now so bulbous, they burst and fill the woman-throats with more fresh slime. The taste is different, for the dead man has just ejaculated. Orgasmed into oblivion. The women take turns in mounting the meat.

Bending over the face, they suck out the eyes and tongue them carefully into each others' vaginas. Biting off the balls, they gob them into the empty eye sockets. Lifting arm-sized pieces of driftwood, the women smash the head of the animal. Brain the colour of vomit leaks out from the sides of the skull. The rampant females eat greedily of the mush, until the entire cranial contents churn violently in the acid of their stomachs. Reaching from behind the boulder, they produce a fang-sharp knife with which they slit open the belly, causing the innards to spill out in a mess of steam. They fling the tortuous guts upon the open ocean, where they twist and curl in the warm darkness. Then they strip off the skin and feed it to the crazed night eels. Rushing to the water's edge, they slither in beneath an incoming crest. As the blood, shit and spunk ease off from their white limbs, they come together and make love in screaming orgasmic reds upon the black sand. The priest's voice was low like a prayer as it urged her to repent and to repeat countless rosaries over and over again.

"Father, I have sinned. I have been with a man who is not my husband. I have been with a man who is sealed in wedlock to another. I have given shelter to devils in my arse. I have never done anything like this, before. I feel... dirty. I am a whore. I am a snake."

The voice was silent. Listening. She was able to make out the faint outline of a face but beyond that, nothing.

"I feel there will be no end to this. Once I have let go, there will be no end to the... sin. I am afraid, Father and yet... and yet, I want it. There has never been anything I desire more in my life than to wallow in the excesses of the sins of the flesh. Why is it so, Father?"

The voice was silent. Dark shadows writhed around the faceless face.

Teasing. Tormenting. Tempting.

She got up and stepped out of the box. Lifting her hand to the curtain, she drew it across. Light flooded in, exposing the priest inside. He squinted in the bright, merciless light. His hand was wrapped around his phallus, which was bulging and purple with the years of masturbation and frustrated desire. He was not old. Perhaps

Melanie Desmoulins

thirty. A waste of a life, Lucy thought, as she knelt down before the Man of God. His eyes wore fear like a cassock. She comforted him and moved her lips around the tumescence of his organ. He closed his eyes and his head fell back against the wood. The curtain was wide open, but she didn't care. Gradually allowing her mouth to become filled up with the bulging mass of flesh, she worked at the base with her thumb and index finger, and began to suck on the dome. She tasted the purity of thirty virgin years. The phallus was the stiffest she had ever come across. She felt it force its hard flesh up against her palate. She wanted to gag. His pre-come squirted onto the back of her mouth. She tasted the clear liquid. She savoured its purity. She pumped his balls. She would be his first. She would be his Eve. His loins stiffened. He groaned. He roared. The boiling shot filled her mouth within seconds. And still he kept coming. She did not swallow any of it. She wanted to savour every last drop. When at last, the holy fucker sank back, dry and fellated, with one last suck she drew out the end-drops of his come. She moved up and kissed him on the lips, the spunk still in her mouth. She had not spilled a drop of the chaste liquid. As she left the house of god, she leaned over the chalice which contained the holy water and spat into it, a stream of sour silver. The spunk, mixed with her own saliva, made strange, curling patterns in the clear lake. She saw her face.

The face of the whore.

As she left the confessional, Lucy bent to kiss the priest's ring. Two rings. He pulled his hand away. She ran from the House Of God. She had absolution but it was an empty cleansing. A fake purity. Like those virgins who, once deflowered went to have their hymens re-made so as to prove to their husbands that they had always been maidens, after all. She could never be re-cast in the image of what she was before.

It was another day dipped in perfect Aragonese blue. Lucy clambered up over the rocks and scrub towards the peak of the plateau which towered like a giant's shoulder above the town. Perspiration ran in beads down her face and her breath came in short gasps as she struggled for a foothold amidst the dust and stone of Mesquita Mountain. She had decided that exercise – and a lot of it – would be the best way to purge herself of the debauchery of her senses. Physical exercise had always been prescribed by the ancients – who ought to have known – as a remedy against all kinds of malaise. Something had slipped within her mind and spirit since she had come south. She wasn't entirely sure, why. Perhaps it was the change of scene – no-one knew her in these parts and what she did wouldn't matter in three weeks' time. Maybe it was the break, after years of labour and loss and the monotony of respectability. She could feel the passing away of sorrow, the death of death, and it made her feel guilty. But it was none of these things and the loosening of her spirit was simply a consequence of the broad Atlantic blue and the heady mixture of freshest Vinho Verde and honeyed Brandymel liquor. And yet, it was all of these things. The sun, already powerful as a Portuguese wrestler, beat down upon her brow, making her thoughts run into one another with the ocean rollers. Just keep climbing, she thought, just keep climbing.

She had almost reached the top. Beneath her feet she could almost feel the flat palm of the plateau which looked in one direction over town and sea and in the other, back toward the hinterlands almost all the way to the Alemtejo where, in a flip of the sun's eyelid, Moors and the Counts of Christendom had fought long and bloody battles. She would sit upon the plateau and she would drink some water and eat some of the bread and mountain goat's cheese which she had brought with her.

Just then, she heard voices.

There was nothing unusual about that – many people climbed this hill, even at this time of year. But she stopped, nonetheless. She didn't know why. Something inside her, some animal instinct, impelled her to halt. Her breath fell as she tried to listen, tried to make out what was being said. It was something in the tone of the voices – not relaxed or merry as one might expect but insistent, compelling, sinister. The voices issued from the dark night in Lisbon down some old Moorish alleyway with the sticky heat of August coating everything, even sound, with its all-or-nothing passion. They were hissing like snakes. The conversation was out of place here in the open mountain morning air in the Spring of almond blossom and oranges, high above the clear blue of the endless Atlantic. The voices belonged to a man and woman. They were speaking in Portuguese but here and there, the occasional word of English was thrown in. She listened for several minutes, trying to make herself inaudible as the sky, invisible as the air. Suddenly her foot slipped, sending a small cascade of dust and stone rolling down the hillside. The voices stopped. Lucy held her breath. She perched behind the trunk of an old almond tree. It would not be thick enough to hide her body so she crouched down as low as she could. She let her breath out slowly as the conversation resumed with somewhat more urgency than before. The voices seemed familiar. The woman began to whisper with an angry rasp. Lucy wished she were able to understand what they were saying. The man continued in a monotone voice as if, by his very composure he were taunting the woman. Lucy thought she heard Antonio's name coming up, again and again. The woman began to shout. Then suddenly, the voices stopped. She heard footsteps move away. She reasoned they must be descending by the other path – the one which led straight down into the town. She decided to wait there for a few minutes longer before venturing out. She turned around and rested her tired back against the smoothness of the tree-trunk. She closed her eyes and let the sun pour down over her face. She really had to try and relax. All this crazy paranoia. She'd heard two people arguing and instantly, it was to do with her. She chuckled. What a fool she'd been! Suddenly, from behind the tree came the sound of footsteps. Someone was running towards her. Her body tensed. She was unable to move. A woman ran past, not noticing Lucy at all. The man was not with her. The woman was weeping. Lucy was unable to quite make out who she was but glancing out from behind the corner of the bushes, she thought she recognized the bowed back of Rachel. She was on her knees, sobbing loudly. Her cries were unrestrained, like those of an animal. And yet there was more than that, there was a grief deeper than any beast could know, there was a blade of fire which no dumb creature could have felt. Lucy had the mindless urge to rush up and comfort the woman, to put her arms around her and hush her cries, one woman to another. After a few minutes, Rachel fell silent. She got up, adjusted her dress and walked slowly down the hillside. It seemed perverse, but somehow the silence was more galling than the obscene bellowing of just a few moments earlier. Lucy could bear it no longer and she emerged from the bushes. Turning in the opposite direction from that which the woman had taken, she made her way up the last few yards to the summit and stood looking out over the bay. A soft breeze with just the sliver of a chill blew her hair into disarray and she ran her hand through the strands, letting the cool air stroke across her forehead, easing away the sweat. It was unusually hot, even for this region. Antonio said it had come from Africa, from the Land of the Moors just as they, themselves had once streamed across in their ships. And when they had left, the mark of their palm had remained. This place seemed strange to her, alien in many ways. It was closer to Africa than to the Europe she had known or imagined. It was drawing out things from deep within her which she had never before thought existed. She trembled slightly and drew her arms around her breasts. You never really knew yourself – not really, not until you were placed in a situation... you just wore a series of skins, and that became what you thought of as yourself. She had never really known Peter, before or after. She gulped the clean air of the plaino, of the ceramic sky, of the rustling sea, of the dunes of Africa. She had come up here to exorcise those demons which the Al Gharb, the land of the west had drawn forth, she had striven up onto this plateau above the hot city to see herself from the outside, to watch time move over the ocean and yet in so doing, she had merely been drawn ever more tightly into their web. Antonio's name had kept coming up. She was almost sure the man with the monotone voice had been Bartolomeo and that Rachel was involved with him in some way. Perhaps he was blackmailing her. But Rachel didn't seem the sort of woman whom it would be possible to blackmail. Blackmail worked on shame, and she had none. Bartolomeo. Such a man would bury himself during the summer, creeping about at night like a bat. The short Algarvan winter was his time. She shuddered again. It wasn't as hot as it seemed. The cold here could slip unseen into your bones and kill you before you knew it. Perhaps he aroused something deep in Rachel's booze-laden brain. But then, Antonio had also appealed to her, hadn't he? Once on a day. Strange, how people are. You never even know yourself. Until it is too late.

She sat down on a rock and watched, far below as the tide came in. She felt herself drawn relentlessly inwards, to this place, to this man, to herself. There would be no escaping. Not today, not ever.

δδδδδδδδδδδδδ

The next morning, she was sitting on the terrace glancing through some newspapers when a waiter came up to her and said something in broken English. He saw that she did not understand and pointed first to her and then at the chair opposite.

"...mar. Mar..."

Lucy continued to gaze distractedly at him.

"What? Sea? What sea?"

Again he pointed at the chair.

"*Nao morte, nao morte.*"

"What??" Lucy was becoming exasperated.

"What are you talking about?"

But he threw his hands up and cleared away the dishes. She wished she could understand Portuguese. It was such a damned difficult language. She tried to fall back into the paper.

A man rushed up to her. It was Antonio. He sat down, right on the chair which the waiter had been pointing at, a moment before. There was an urgency in his expression.

"Lucy. I need to talk to you."

She did not answer. His face, which she had tried not to look at, was unshaven and framed by tousled strands of black hair. He looked as if he'd been up all night.

"It's Rachel. She tried to kill herself."

The paper dropped into her lap.

"...What?"

"She walked into the sea. Last night. She had been drinking, and she just walked into the sea. A fisherman saved her. The tide was coming in."

"...But, why?"

Lucy was unable to decide whether it was relief, or disappointment she heard in his voice. She shivered. The morning was chilly.

He looked up at her.

"Who knows? The drink, her life, the demon that writhes within her... who knows?"

"Has she done this before?"

He nodded.

"But not as close. This time was very close. I think she meant it, this time."

Lucy reached out across the table and touched his hand.

"Oh, Antonio..."

The Snake

She squeezed his hand. He was limp, cold. A thought occurred to her.

"It's not... it's not because of us, is it? I mean, she didn't do it because of us?"

He sighed.

"...Who knows? Who knows what goes on in her mind? I thought I knew, once. That was a long time ago. A whole life ago."

Lucy felt suddenly sick. She pulled her hand away.

"If I thought it was because of us..."

"Then, what?" he demanded sharply, "Then what? Why should we live our lives in fear of what she might or might not do, of what people might or might not say? We all must plot our own course through the waves, or drown."

He stopped abruptly.

"I'm sorry, Lucy. I can't help it. When I heard about her, I wished she had..."

She grabbed his hand and pulled him to her.

"Don't say it. I understand. I couldn't get you out of my head. I tried, but I couldn't."

They kissed. His lips were cold and they trembled. She eased her own lips around his, comforting, warm, loving and at length he relaxed them and began to grow passionate.

"I missed you," he began but she cut him off with another kiss, and another and another.

"Let's go somewhere else," she suggested.

"...my room."

Slowly, carefully, with a skill she had not been aware she possessed, she peeled off his clothes. She tickled his hairless chest, his muscular limbs, his firm torso. She brought his tired arms up over her shoulders and let him smooth her skin. His hands were soft like butter. She played her slim fingers around his lips. He bit her fingers and then sucked them, allowing his eyes to close. He began to be roused and ran his palms up and down along her spine and over her trembling haunches. She felt that her heart would leap out of her chest and yet, she wanted to prolong the agony, to die a thousand times in his arms. As if he were a sexual conjurer, he ran the tips of his fingers over her nipples, drawing them taut. The magician drew her chest upwards to meet his. Her eyes were closed. She felt her whole body unite with one desire, a feeling beyond thought, beyond guilt, beyond shame. Her spine tingled with primitive need, her toes wanted to splay out and run over the bare backs of sand and rock, her soles to feel the cut and blood of shells and stone. She smoothed his wavy hair with her palms and clutched at his ears. He cupped his hands beneath her buttocks and drew her to him. She felt the male pressure of his force inch between her legs, quivering like the throat of a bird along the swollen, moist forest of her lips. Still, she wanted to postpone the joy, still she longed for pain and for his teeth to tear her heart from its very root and squeeze the blood slowly from her body. With his tumescence, he teased her feminine desire, turning her round and round so that the room spun with her lust and it spread and flowed over the entire face of the sky with its shameless moans. He sensed her need for this to go on and he too, held back. When she did fall slowly from the sky, he was waiting for her as he had waited since the dawn of time, as he had lain back upon his elbow in fields of orchid and light and waited for her, as he had lain on the bottom of the sea with the stones smooth as skin and the strange, one-eyed sexless fish and waited for her. And when she did come down and thrust him deep into her, he let out a moan of animal pleasure and he dug his nails into the soft firmness of her buttocks, drawing her around him, urging her onwards, She moved slowly, slower than slow, and he moved with her. She felt a warmth arise from deep within her body, from somewhere between the small of her back and the small of her love cushion. She held it back for as long as she could, moving slow, so slow, almost not-moving. But the force of her passion was too great. She knew she must let go this time. For she had reached the shore and with the tide had come this man whom she wanted, desired, needed... She thrust herself all around him, the tidal waves of her body erupting over him, covering his male fire with a soft balm, easing the pain with gentleness, moving over the shallows and the deeps and the strange, one-eyed fish and the white, skin-smooth stones and the blue, flat-faced sky. She was the bow of the oldest violin in the world, she was the arrow of desire's string, she was the unravelling of rope, she was finally and wonderfully, queen of everything, empress of herself. She let out a scream as she felt him go taut beneath her. Their cries mingled as the heaven of their fulfilment went on without end. When at last, she slumped down across his chest, he did not withdraw but stayed in her as if that were the way it had always been, as if they had always been, one. She knew that they could never now be anything else.

They did not speak till they had showered and dressed.

"I'm leaving her."

"After all this time? After what happened last night?"

"I should have done it years ago. But sometimes, you think a crippled, twisted thing is better than nothing at all. My love for Rachel was not real. It was just pity. Pity and perversion, maybe. Fuck her. Fuck her to Hell."

"How can love not be real? What about me? What is that?"

He looked at her. His face had grown fresh compared to earlier that morning.

"You are not the same. One cannot compare..."

There was a pause as the sound of a scooter whizzing past blotted out thought for a moment.

"You must stay with me. You must not go back to England. For there lies only death. And here, without you, there is nothing."

"My family will think I'm mad. Perhaps, I am. But it's a lovely madness, a wonderful insanity and I want it to go on forever. What about your family?"

He chuckled cynically.

"They did not accept her. They will not accept you. To them, all Englishwomen are the same. Perhaps my grandmother... she's different, she has lived too long. But it makes no difference, what they think. It makes no difference what your family think. We are together. That is all that matters."

The room lit up yellow as the sun splashed in through the slatted blinds.

They left the hotel and drove out to the country, to the hills around Silves and beyond, where the air is clearer, the sky closer to the earth. And when night fell, they went to his house and they lay upon the cold tiles of the drawing-room before the warm hearth-fire and he peeled off her clothes and opened a bottle of finest Port and warmed it before the fire. And when it was good and burning, he rubbed it all over her thighs and her shoulders. And he licked the hot red wine from her skin and he thrust his tongue deep into her mouth and she tasted the burning grape blood and he moved so fast he burned the insides of her knees. And in the flames, she burned three, four times that night. Her arsehole, a winding, spiralling staircase of delight. A grinning, pulsating bordello of freedom. And they slept and woke and slept and woke and when at last, utterly exhausted they sank together into the warm balm of darkness, in the moment just before all thought was extinguished, Lucy thought she heard the sound of a foghorn somewhere out upon the endless ocean.

seven

Green peas, boiled carefully with onions, and powdered with cinnamon, ginger and cardamoms, well-pounded, create for the consumer considerable amorous passion and strength in coitus.

The sun grew hotter as the days flipped through the March month. Lucy had spent the morning browsing around some small shops and was now picking her way across some large rocks which skirted a small peninsula. Suddenly the sound of footsteps came from behind her. Before she could turn around to see who it was, a hand grabbed her blouse and shook her violently. Another hand pushed her hard, almost causing her to overbalance and fall into the sea. She collapsed onto her knees and twisted around. A fist struck her on the left jaw and again on the right. She looked up. The woman's face was that of a witch, red and swollen with booze and anger. Hatred sprang like a dog from her eyes. She was barely recognisable.

"Rachel," Lucy blurted out as a third punch split her upper lip.

"You bitch!" the woman screamed, "You bitch!! I'm going to send you to away forever. I'll make it so you can never look at a man again."

Her breath smelled like vomit.

Lucy held up her hands to shield her face. The woman almost lost her footing as she swung punches at Lucy's head. Instinctively, Lucy reached forward and grabbed her by the heels. She tugged with all her might. The woman screamed and fell backwards. Lucy got up and flung herself on top of the struggling figure. With her knees she pinned her to the ground. She slapped her three times. Hard. The woman looked surprised. Suddenly sober.

Melanie Desmoulins

"Don't you dare touch me again. Antonio loves me, not you. He hates you. He always has. You're a drunk, a stinking drunk. You should be dead. You should be with that pale pervert. You're finished. If I see you again, I'll kill you."

Lucy found herself frothing at the lips. She gave the woman another slap and got up. Removing the black belt from her dress, she slipped it beneath Rachel's groin. She ran it back and forth across the bitch's cunt, across the beast's hard clit. She would make the tart want her. She would make her into a handmaiden. A lesbian companion. An extension of her own clit, and nothing more. She would bruise her female arse. She would run her long, thin, white fingers up the other woman's arsehole until the bitch screamed for mercy. Yelled from joy. Yes! Yes! Yes! Now Lucy was on top. Now Lucy was the goddess of sex. The belt grew wet with the uncontrollable desire of the woman. The animal need. Rachel moaned and threw back her neck. Grabbing her long, black hair, Lucy forced her head down even further. She banged the tart's skull off the hard rock below, until it bled from behind. She would dash her brains out and then eat them, raw. Yes! Yes! Yes! As she walked back towards the town, she felt the itch of blood upon her chin. She wiped it away. She was trembling inside. And yet, within the trembling, there was a force which grew and filled up her body so that she felt no pain, no shame. She was strong, stronger than ever. She knew she could do anything. As she swaggered away, the shape of Rachel's body made a sensuous curve upon the earth. She had the sudden desire to rape her, to perform a lesbian rape on the woman, to shock the unshockable, to rub her cunt over the bitch's mouth and make her a part of herself. Who said violence was only for men? She pushed the thought away with some difficulty. Something was happening to her. She was changing. Or maybe this was what she had always been. A bitch. A hot, tribadic bitch. Mother-Of-One. Well, fuck her. Lucy could fuck Rachel, could smear herself all over the bitch, could stick a smooth metal penis into her and make come in spite of herself. All those wasted, suburban years. All those damn nice people. They were surely damned. She would lie with whom she wanted and create a race of beasts without the awful shackle of morals around her arsehole. Go and fuck whom thy wishest to fuck, go and lie with that which thou wishest to lie, go and be merry, for Satan's sake, for thine own sake. Because what does it matter, in the long run. Who the fuck remembers who was fucked by whom, in the year 2000? No-one. No bloody one. Who remembers who was good, and who was bad? No-one. No body. No mind. No soul. Let the Devil take the hindmost. Damn all the popes. Il Papa. Fuck them all. Lucy would ride them like she had ridden Antonio, like she had ridden Rachel, the prime bitch. Let her drink, eat and be orgasmic all the time like one of those lucky bloody liver-flukes. Spent their whole lives in climax. There were not words enough in her mind to express the joys of pure animal satisfaction that coursed through her body. Through the blood of her lips, through the stink of her wet cunt, her long legs – yes, she had long, sensuous legs which any man, woman or beast would crave to kiss, rub, be entwined in – long, white, legs, the seductors of emperors and whores, alike. When was the last time a whore sucked the joys of sex? Never, probably. It was just a job, a profession. The oldest. The vocation of the cunt. Bad. Good. Lucy was wiser than that. She wanted sex for enjoyment. She didn't need the money. Antonio's money was hers. She would never have to work again. Ha! Fuck all you poor suckers. Just get a man with enough to feed your mouth and your cunt, and that would be enough. Her clit was throbbing with the power of her power. She wanted to go back and make Rachel her slave, her lesbian concubine. There was a purity in the love of one woman, for another. Rachel wanted her. She knew that. And she wanted Rachel, she wanted her slack-mouthed whore mouth. She wanted to out-Rachel, Rachel. O God! O Satano! O Satano-godo! She felt the sangria which she had been consuming too much of seep into her soul and break it apart, bit by English bit. The joy of the pure whiteness of her Anglo-Saxon spirit flooded through her body. She ruled the earth. She could have anything she wanted, any man, any woman, any beast. She had won the world and the world was hers. With her cunt and her ass had she conquered the earth, and Lucy felt the pride of her race sink into her desire. She could do anything.

δδδδδδδδδδδδ

"How did you get that cut? And that black eye?" Antonio asked, with a look of concern.

"...Guess."

He shook his head.

"...Rachel?"

She nodded slowly. It hurt to nod quickly.

He slammed his fist down upon the table.

"Bitch! I'll kill her!"

Lucy reached out and touched his hand, wrapping her palm around his fine, long fingers.

"No, darling, you won't. You'll do nothing. Absolutely nothing. That's what she wants – for you to get angry and do something. For us to worry about what she'd going to do next. We are together. That's what we want. That's all that matters. Leave her to rot. She's just a drunk."

He looked her in the eye. For a moment, she thought she detected surprise in his look, as if he didn't believe she could be so strong, so offhand. As if he didn't really know her. But then, she hadn't really known herself. Not really. Not inside.

"I gave her something to remember. I don't think she'll bother us again."

"You don't know the jealousy of women."

"Oh yes I do. Anyway, she's not a woman. She's a creature. A nothing."

"She's living with that... disgusting man."

"Then she deserves him."

"I told her."

"I know."

She smiled.

"Really, darling. How can you not have noticed? When she's not drunk, she's stoned and sometimes, she's both. She pays him with money... and with her body – what's left of it – and he gives her what she needs."

A look of sorrow passed over his face, and than it was gone. But just before it vanished, Lucy thought she detected surprise behind the sorrow.

"My marriage... was a lie. A lie. My family were right."

"...About her, they were. But I am not her."

He looked up and smiled. His half-moon lips, his soft, wondrous lips. He squeezed her hand.

"No, my darling, you're not."

They kissed. Her lips hurt.

"I love you," she moaned through the pain, "I will always

love you."

δδδδδδδδδδδδ

They drove along the coast to a deserted beach which, Antonio had said, would be filled with hidden coves. They climbed down three hundred-and-twenty-seven steps – Lucy counted every one – and he led her to the deepest recess in the entire cliff-face. They lay down on the sand. From here, they could see the ocean waves flowing ever inward, crowned by the upturned shell of the sky. The sun was hidden by the enormous dark overhang of rock which lay above them. The sand was warm. She made him crouch on all fours, legs widely spread so that his soft, glistening arsehole lay exposed to the cooling evening air. She began to lick him around its margins, making the crumpled mouth pout and gleam with mucous. She thrust her thumb into his arse. He let out a cry of pain and joy. Massaging the shit-hole, she pulled out her thumb and inserted her index and middle fingers right up to the knuckles. He moaned. She began to massage the bulging gland inside while, with her other hand, she pumped his balls mercilessly. They were so hard in her palm, she felt that they would burst. Pre-come dripped from the end of his stalk. Everything grew tight. The arsehole clamped its lips around her fingers like the jaws of a snake. His dirt cavern screamed at her.

Please please please please please please please please please!!!!!

When he came, it was with the force of a bull. With each spurt of come, a cry escaped his mouth. The hot spunk spurted from his cock for a full minute. By the time he'd finished, a large pool of it lay glinting in the dying sunlight. They lay for a while. No words passed between them. Using her lips and tongue, she pulled back his foreskin and began to lick the bulging glans. A speck of glistening pre-come appeared from its thin slit, and she greedily lapped this onto the tip of her tongue. It tasted sweet. Then, bit by bit, she took more and more of the pulsating organ into her hot mouth. She began to suck – gently at first, then more forcefully – and Antonio groaned and threw back his head. Now she was sucking with all the might of her cheeks and neck. She could feel the balls harden against her chin. With a shout, he came into her mouth. He pumped and pumped, and again it seemed as though he would never stop. She felt the delicious, burning spunk slither down her throat. He rolled over onto her and she felt the roughness of a man's back, she felt him arch like a tree in a hurricane. He whispered in her ear:

"Before you, there was nothing. My life was empty like a dry jug."

She felt her head in the close air beneath the rock. She tried to straighten out her thoughts, to make them walk in single file, one after the next.

"...But there was Rachel."

"Ah, forget that. Don't talk of that. It is finished."

His voice was loving but firm.

So she said nothing more and simply enjoyed the pleasures of having a man again, she felt the rough bark of rapturous idiocy scrape past her as she sank ever deeper into him, until she could see no way out, no means of escape. And anyway, she wasn't sure she wanted to.

ẟẟẟẟẟẟẟẟẟẟẟẟ

Antonio was in his study, poring over some paperwork when she burst in.

"Bastard!"

She threw down her handbag. It clattered onto the tile floor. She stood, hands-on-hips, her face smudged in old rouge. He felt his eye drawn to her lower lip which was overhanging slightly like the tress of a whore. He turned back to his desk.

"Look at me when I'm talking to you!" she yelled.

"Give me that much respect."

He wheeled slowly towards her.

"Respect should be earned."

She wagged her finger.

"Listen – get rid of that bitch, or I'll..."

"What? What will you do?"

"If I go down, you go down. I'll drag your name through the mud. No-one will touch you or your business, again. You'll be ruined."

He shrugged.

"You have been messing me about for years."

"That's different."

"How?"

He laughed, cynically.

"Don't put on that stupid laugh. I may come from the gutter but so do you. I know everything about you, and more."

"Do you, now?"

There was a strange pause, an unintended gap.

"OK – how is it different?"

"That's just playing around. I never loved any of them. Like you with that girl from Porto. She was just a toy. We agreed that's how it would be. It was part of the deal – or have you forgotten that, too."

"That was a long time ago."

"Oh, I see. So when it comes to you, it doesn't apply. How very convenient!"

He began to lose his cool.

"What about the drink? The drugs? That was not in our 'agreement'. When you come home stinking like a bottle of port, do you expect me to just sit here and take it?"

She smiled coyly, like a trained coquette.

"I thought you liked port."

He shuffled awkwardly.

"Oh, so prim and proper now, are we? Have you tried it on her, yet."

"Shut up."

"You have, haven't you?"

Her smile broadened into a grin.

"Did she like it?"

"I said shut up!"

"Did she moan like me?"

"Shut up, you drunken bitch!"

Her smile vanished like that of a madman.

"Why do you think I started drinking?"

"Why? I don't know. I really don't know. And I don't bloody care."

Her face sagged and a shadow fell across her. She seemed suddenly ten years older.

"When you stopped loving me."

Melanie Desmoulins

"Our marriage has been dead for years."

She looked up again.

"This woman is different, isn't she?"

There was a pause as the clicking sound of grasshoppers opened up beyond the trellised window.

"Yes. She is different. I love her."

Rachel's eyes grew moist as he went on.

"I have learned that one can love without conditions. That is why she is different."

"But she goes back in a week!"

He paused again. Beneath the insect noise, her heart dropped in its sac.

"No, she's not."

A hole opened up in the air where her heart had been.

"I asked her to stay."

Rachel's mouth opened, then closed again like that of a drunken fish.

"You can't... how can you?"

"I have. I'm sick of you and your booze and your damn drugs. Go to Bartolomeo. He is your type. You are the walking dead. I choose to be with the living."

He turned his back on her. She seemed deflated. He heard her sloppy footsteps recede toward the door. Then suddenly she ran up behind him and brought a poker down on his head. He realised too late and tried to swerve sideways. The heavy metal rod caught him on the ear and fell down on his neck and he felt the world go fuzzy.

The grasshoppers grew louder and filled up the world's air with their bellowing.

ꙮꙮꙮꙮꙮꙮꙮꙮꙮꙮ

Antonio awoke and saw Lucy's face.

"How are you, darling?"

He tried to move his mouth, but his ear hurt when he did this, so he gave up. As if sensing this, she put her finger to his lips.

"Don't talk, dear. Just rest."

He was in a hospital bed. Light streamed in through the enormous windows as if heaven had come at last to rest upon the earth. In spite of her advice and his pain, he managed to force out the words:

"...What happened?"

"Don't you remember?"

He didn't answer.

"Someone hit you over the head. You're lucky to be here. 'Only superficial wounds,' they said. The odd thing is, nothing was taken. Nothing was stolen."

She paused.

"Antonio. Who was it?"

He looked her straight in the eye.

"...her?"

He was silent.

"You were talking in your sleep. Something about paintings, black water, white men. It sounded very odd."

She took hold of his hand and squeezed it.

"Antonio. Was it her? Tell me. You can tell me."

He tried to turn his head away but it hurt too much.

"Why are you protecting her?"

Lucy strove to keep the anger out of her voice.

"We should press charges. We..."

He lifted up his hand to silence her.

"...No. I am guilty. She has her justice. I loved her, once."

Lucy turned away, a look of dismay and anger on her face. She was unable to restrain herself.

"You still do."

He took her arm, pulling her back round.

"I love you. Only you."

"Then press charges. It's the only way. Otherwise she'll never stop. She is dangerous. Unbalanced. God knows what she will do next. You must... for me, if not for yourself."

He shook his head.

Lucy sighed with frustration.

Closing his eyes, he fell back against the pillow. The bandage around his head felt tight, throttling. A thudding ache began to pound behind his eyes. He sank back into a sleep without dreams.

Rachel had vanished.

Her clothes were missing and so was she. Antonio refused

to press charges. The police said he was mad, the cleaner who'd found him lying in a pool of blood was of the same mind as the police and Lucy agreed with both of them. Bartolomeo too, seemed to have disappeared. It were as if the two of them had simply faded into the dense wall of booze and drugs and despair which they had spent years erecting around themselves. Lucy phoned her daughter that night and explained that she was not returning on her scheduled flight. She was met with silence. Finally, her daughter's voice said:

"...But, why? I don't understand."

"Jane, I've tried to explain to you. I have met someone. Ever since your father died, I've been... well, you know what I've been like. I've met this wonderful man – Antonio – and he makes me feel I want to live again. After all these years."

"But, mum..."

"Try to understand. There will never be a replacement for Peter. No-one could replace your father. You know that. But I cannot feel guilty all my life. I am entitled to a little happiness, am I not?"

"But you had coped so well... after father died."

"That's it – I coped. I didn't live. There's a difference, you know."

"No-one's talking about guilt."

"That's the problem – no-one talks about it."

There was a pause.

"...But your job..."

"I'm going to meet his people, his family, tomorrow. He has money – not that it's important to us. I love him, and that's that. Please, try and understand. You should come out to meet him. You would get on..."

"But when are you coming home? What about your job? Your house? Us?"

"You mean, 'What about you?'"

Silence again.

"I'll sell the house. Come and meet him, Jane. Then you'll understand. I'm not coming back. Not to live. This is my home, now."

Silence.

"...It's not so far away," she pleaded and then felt angry that she should feel the need to plead before her own daughter.

As she walked back to Antonio's house, she felt sad that Jane still did not understand. It would take time. Anyway, she thought with a sense of elation, she didn't care what they felt. Her family, her so-called friends, her work... they all had their own lives. They were in her past. If she had died under a bus, they would all be getting on with it by now, so why shouldn't she? She didn't interfere with them, so why should they poke their long, disapproving noses into her life? She was happy. She deserved that, after all she'd been through, surely. Why was she trying to defend herself, to herself? She shouldn't feel guilty. Why should she? There was nothing wrong in what she was doing. Over the years, Rachel had forfeited any rights she might've had over Antonio and now finally, by this assault, she had no claim on him whatsoever. Lucy found herself smiling in the dark. Now that's something the old Lucy, the boring old English Lucy would never have done. Always trying to please everyone, so they wouldn't think badly of her, so they wouldn't get angry. And where had all that ingratiating behaviour got her? She'd painted herself right into the goody-goody corner, from which there is no escape, lest it be death or...

She was still angry at Antonio for not pressing charges. It meant he still felt something for Rachel. On some level, some deep level which she had not yet reached, he still loved her. That's what enraged her. There was something she was not getting about all of this. Something which was eluding her. Lucy wanted that bitch to feel the wroth of her justice, she wanted to jump her from behind and tear out her eyes, slit her nipples with long nails, make her cower and beg for mercy. Like a pig. Like a bloody pig! She shuddered at such thoughts. Strange, how one can live one's life, thinking never an extreme thought. And then, an overwhelming emotion comes along, be it love, hate or envy – or perhaps all three – and anyone, anyone can be pushed – no, would rush – to the brink. To adultery, sodomy, murder and beyond.

Outside, the clouds were gathering. The strange heatwave was over. The warm currents of air which had blown from the African desert were being forced into retreat by the ice winds of Galicia. Up in the north of the country, in Porto and Braga, the cold fingers of contrition were clasping one another beneath a darkening sky while the seamless ocean began to mass in great, grey rollers upon the land's rim. And at length, even down in the sheltered coves

Melanie Desmoulins

of Algarve, winter would return to reclaim his natural right to earth and sky.

ठठठठठठठठठठठ

They drove all night toward the hills. As they climbed ever higher, the air grew colder until Antonio had to switch on the car heater and Lucy wrapped herself in thick woollens and yet still felt chilly. As dawn's pale light spread itself reluctantly over the land, Lucy could see that things were utterly different on this side of the mountains. Winter had never left the high plateau which for centuries had been known as 'The Empty Country', and the sun shone cold like the edge of a diamond high up in the deep blue. This was the Alemtejo. People here were a good deal less well-off than in the prosperous, fertile Algarve and the countryside looked as though fire and ice had raged over its flat chest for centuries. The scrub there was, did little to break the sepia monotony of the high plaino. The occasional tractor or even herd of cattle merely served to accentuate the loneliness of this vast province. It was the merciless country, a malevolent land which had burned for centuries in its unending fire. Antonio had told her that this was where the Portuguese soul had been forged. This must be where all those intrepid explorers had got their backbone. Prince Henry The Navigator, Vasco Da Gama, Bartolomeo Diaz... Lucy fell asleep, dreaming of wooden ships and strange, angular knights tilting lances at windmills...

They arrived with a jolt. Antonio gestured towards a small, white cottage lying at the far end of a track.

"...My grandmother's house."

There was a pride in his voice that belied the diminutive size of the dwelling. She felt her heart leap with anticipation. What would she think of her? What would the spawn of this forbidding landscape think of her, another Englishwoman come to beguile and steal away their son?

They went up to the door. A small, silver-haired woman dressed all in black was waiting for them by the open doorway. She resembled Antonio only in her eyes and nose and in something around the mouth. The same long, perfect nose, the same glint in her eye. It was the glint of the stars of the early evening as they rose in the sky. She greeted Antonio in a stream of Portuguese and seemed at first to ignore Lucy altogether. At last, Antonio introduced them and she cast her shining eyes upon the Englishwoman's face. With a quick glance, she had her sized up. Lucy shivered in the cool morning air but tried desperately to conceal this as she shook hands with the old matriarch. On her left hand, she wore a serpent ring. Antonio seemed to ask her something. She led them to two bedrooms, clearly indicating to Lucy that she would sleep in a separate room from Antonio. Lucy fired a glance at Antonio but he seemed not to notice. There seemed to be Crosses everywhere. There were more Crosses than in a church. Lucy slumped down on the bed and despite the strange surroundings, she fell asleep almost at once. Her sleep was without dreams.

When she awoke, it was to the sound of loud knocking. Antonio whispered loudly through the door.

"Get up, it's time to eat."

It was already dark. Then she realised she must have slept all through the day. During the simple meal, the grandmother was polite but cold. Lucy was left feeling empty. She was silent on the drive back.

"I sense you are uneasy. You must understand. She is very traditional. She had a bad experience with Rachel and now she is worried once again. She doesn't know who you are. She is afraid. She will come round. Give her time."

He glanced sideways at her.

"...You'll see."

Lucy returned his look but then turned to look at the almond blossom as it flurried past her window. The white flowers of hope in the midst of darkness.

They turned right down a long track. Lucy didn't remember coming this way but as again it was night, she couldn't be certain. The land all looked the same.

Suddenly the car stopped.

Antonio turned to her.

"What is it?" she asked.

"You know what it is. This must be sorted out now. Family is very important to us Portuguese. It's not like England..."

"Fine. So if the Family is the most important thing, then why bother about me...?"

Her voice broke. She turned away.

Melanie Desmoulins

He leaned across and slipped his arm around her but she pushed him away.

"Lucy..." he urged, soothingly. "Lucy, I love you. You are the most wonderful thing that has happened to me in my life."

He paused.

"That is why I am bothered about you. Family is important, but it is as nothing in the face of love."

She turned back. Tears were streaming down her fac, and were glistening in the starlight.

"You mean that? You wouldn't hurt me. Don't hurt me. Please don't..."

He put a finger to her lips. She tasted him through her tears.

He pulled her to him and embraced her tightly. Her face left a wet imprint upon his jacket. She laughed.

"Now your jacket's wet."

He squinted down and then he too, began laughing.

She loved the sound of his laughter. It was deep and warm like the sands of Algarve, like the swaying Atlantic, like the scorching African breeze. He drew her chin towards him. He kissed her fulsome lips, lightly at first, teasing the skin, allowing them to linger with their softness upon her mouth. She felt his powerful fingers on her back. Ripples ran up and down her spine, fearsome waves of lust that made her want to spread her legs in his face, to rub herself all over his shoulders, to impale herself upon him. But she held back, knowing that the pleasure would be all the greater, the longer she penned in her passion. She felt his tongue invade her mouth, the tip probing like the head of an electric eel along the line of her teeth, her gums. The insides of her mouth melted like wax and she sucked his tongue into her head. They chased each other around inside her and then it was her turn. She pushed him back and flicked her tongue back and forth from her mouth to his. He groaned. She felt his palate hard like the swelling between his legs which was beginning to show through his trousers. He held her breasts cupped in his hands and began to tease around the nipples. He unzipped her dress. She could feel his hands tremble as he fumbled with the metal zip. She took hold of his hand.

"Not here," she cautioned.

"Why not? It's deserted, it's dark. Please..."

She let go.

"I've never done this before."

"There is always a first time for everything – no?"

She smiled.

"What would the Family think?"

He grinned. He began to kiss her neck, pecking at first and then sucking at the soft white skin. She let her head fall back, enjoying every movement of his lips. She felt her legs go soft and the ripples moved from her thighs to her breasts to her neck where the kisses had drawn out large red marks.

Suddenly he stopped and motioned towards the rear of the car. The back seat was broad and plush and when she lay down upon it, she could see stars come at her from all directions. The leather felt cool against her naked back. She trembled, ever so slightly. Gently, he removed the rest of her clothing, until she lay utterly naked beneath the blanket of night. Her body seemed to glow in the gentle starlight, for the moon was not yet born. She took off his shirt and ran her hand down into his trousers. He groaned as she found his member, swollen and hard and throbbing with the beat of his heart. Like a wild animal, she ripped off the encumbrance of his clothes and pulled him to her. She whispered in his ear.

"I want you. I want your face, your shoulders, your chest. I want your thighs, your buttocks, your balls, your cock. Especially these. I want to suck them, all three, until they are mush in my mouth. And then I will swallow them and so you will be in me. You will be me."

His breath solid in the cool night air, he parted her thighs and pressed himself against her clit. He bent down and began to flick his tongue-tip over the meeting-point of her lips. Slowly at first, then faster and faster, he teased at the cove of her femininity. She closed her eyes and let out a low moan. She threw her arms out behind her head so that they hit against the cold glass of the sky. With his fingers, he gently brought every part of her body to a level of excitement she had never before imagined. Her feet swung upward and hit the car-roof and she planted her soles firmly on the soft velvet. She felt the warm wetness flow unrestrained from between her legs, she felt like a night flower opening in the darkness. She needed his rod inside her, she desperately desired the thrust of his phallus burning its way into the blood-red cavern of her animal lust. She grabbed his scrotum. The testicles were hard like marbles, like gems, like swollen eggs ready to burst. She crushed his bag within her palm so that he moaned with pain and joy. She pulled the loose skin, grown taut. She wanted to rip the seed from his body without mercy, like the Amazons of old. She wanted to make him groan, to make him scream, she wanted for him to become her slave forever. She ran her fingers along his shaft. It was hot. Burning. It rose further every time she stroked it. She wanted it inside her, deep inside her. She wanted to ram it into her mouth, down her throat, she craved for it between her buttocks, she needed it to thrust itself like a pine-tree into her anus. She wanted to be buggered over and over again. She longed for the heat of its length to lie between her breasts, to come splurting and slashing in her face. But most of all, she hungered for it in her womb, she thirsted for its heaving back upon her swollen clit, she died for the roughness of its skin pushing back the folds of her lips, the ridge of her vagina. But she wanted to die waiting for the moment, and she would worship the moment as if it were a God upon a plinth. She would let her body waste away in the night of its embrace, she would willingly throw herself upon the fire of its body, she would happily drown herself in the ocean of its eternity. She would smash her body again and again upon its unyielding rock in some exquisite torture from the depths of Hell, just to live the moment just to be the moment before the moment. The sound of nightbirds outside the glass of the car did not reach her ears, for she was no longer in their world. Slowly, she pulled back the skin of his organ and slowly, she ran her fingers up and down his verge, the great elephantskin organ of his lust. Her back arched. She drew him into her. He teased at her lips. She groaned, begging him to fuck her, begging for penetration, pleading for him to deflower her like a lotus. She wished he had five penises so she could pull each one into her, all at the same time. One for each of her glistening, hot body-holes. Like an ocean liner, relentless yet elegant he thrust his loins amongst her thighs. She screamed with delight. She gazed into his eyes. His mouth had opened wide, his lips were wet. He bent down and kissed her. He began to move. He was an engine, a boiler on the brink of explosion. With each thrust, she let out a low moan.

O God O God Give me more! Fuck me forever. Make me die, a thousand times and then fuck me again!

The windows had steamed up with the heat of their passion.

He went slow, then fast then slow again, prolonging the joy, stretching the agony. Her legs fell down from the roof and with her knees, she hauled his buttocks in closer. Deeper. His own naked feet pushed against the door, so that he was a battering-ram, straight and hard as he slid over her thighs, her midriff, her breasts. She felt like a whore. She felt wet all the time.

I am the whore. I am the tart. The piece, the bit, the quean.
I am the minx, the jade, the trash. I am the trollop, the trull, the slut.

Now he did not slow down but moved faster and faster. He was panting like a dog and she, moaning beneath him. He was going so fast, her body felt an unrestrainable urge to move against him. They were like two gymnasts, raised impossibly up off the leather, with twitching muscles and ferocious blood. His hands flew out and grabbed hers which were splayed against the window-panes. His body grew stiffer and she felt his penis tauten within her. Freeing her hands, she squeezed his balls. He roared the deep roar of the jungle, the unfettered animal noise of pure joy. Her hand rejoined his. She felt a warmth rippling up through her body, from the tips of her toes to the roots of her hair. Waves of warmth swirled up and down her body until, like a whirlpool they spun on the hot swelling between her legs. The smell of him was all over her and she wallowed in his maleness of his scent. She closed her eyes and in the darkness beyond black, she felt her body disappear and become less than nothing. She felt a joy beyond happiness, a perfect eternity of lust. The fulfilment of the dog desire of her loins. She felt her body smash upon the rocks, she felt the blood ooze from every pore, she felt the excruciating lick of flame upon skin as she immolated herself in the fir, she felt the killing touch of water flow into her lungs as she drowned in the ocean. As the hot spurt of his release pulsed into her womb, as his body stretched to breaking point, as the roar of conquest cut through his vocal cords, she came again and again, so that her orgasm wrapped itself around his and they became, One. At last, he sank down upon her. Their hearts beat hard upon each other's chests as if at any moment, they would burst out and fill the night with a sea of blood. Behind her eyelids, she felt the redness of her heartblood flow over everything.

 δδδδδδδδδδδδ

The pungent stink of petrol on cloth reached Rachel's nostrils, causing them to flare slightly in the dark. She poured the remainder of the can over the elegant drawing-room furniture. The darkness was thicker than oil and Rachel was part of that darkness. She moved with the night, she was its arms and its legs, she was the writhing back waiting for orgasm, she was the open eye of the moon. Just as she had come here from the north and taken up Antonio and his petty dreams, just as she had grown bored with him and his world and had plunged the needle deep into her heart's blood, just as she had run rampant through the loins of the young studs who wandered along the sea's edge wearing erections and stubble and swaggering chests, so now would she perform the final act of love and destruction. Backing away from the house, she pulled out a cigarette lighter from her trouser pocket and flicked off the catch. The breeze was cool – chilly, almost – and the lighter refused to ignite. On the fifth attempt, a small spark exuded from its mouth, and the petrol-soaked taper burst into flame. She had underestimated the rapidity of the explosion and hastily dropped the taper. Fire slid in serpent coils all over the hall. Within minutes, the house was a lantern of light.

δδδδδδδδδδδδ

Antonio sank to his knees as the sight engulfed him. The black wreck which had been his home seemed to grow darker still in the orange-fresh morning. Lucy threw her arms around his shoulders.

"Oh my God. What happened?"

Antonio did not reply, but began to beat his forehead on the hard ground. Blood poured from the jaw-shaped wounds. Lucy pulled him back.

" Stop!! That won't do any good."

"I don't care! Leave me alone!"

She let go but he stopped beating his head. She sat down on the ground and held her own head in her hands. For a while there was silence as the ocean flung itself against the rocks below and the idiot gulls squawked in their blindness.

"It was her."

Lucy started at his words. He went on, "It is her revenge."

He bent down his head and began to sob. Lucy moved

towards him and took his head upon her breast, and so they remained till the sun and moon both had leapt and fallen and the tears lay dry on his face, leaving only the salt glimmer of stars.

ᵹᵹᵹᵹᵹᵹᵹᵹᵹᵹᵹᵹ

Antonio sank into a listless state of half-existence and for weeks, only Lucy's careful nursing prevented a yet greater disaster from befalling him. At times, he was delirious, ranting on about the evils of womankind and albino devils clad all in white. Then for a moment, he would rise to lucidity but would soon grow exhausted in this state, as if somehow reality and concrete form had grown tiresome for him. All through this, neither of them saw nor heard from Rachel. Along with her baleful albino, she had vanished. No body was found in the wreckage of Antonio's house, the investigation revealing merely that doused petrol had been the cause of the blaze. But there was no proof linking the act of arson with Rachel. Her disappearance – proof enough for Lucy, not to mention Antonio's words of accusation on the morning of his sad discovery – seemed merely an annoyance for the police, who were more interested in winding up the file than anything else. With typical cynicism, they seemed to tacitly suspect Antonio himself of being responsible for the fire and viewed his illness as well-acted sham.

As she nursed him back to health, Lucy felt her love grow from mere exotic lust to something else. Her feelings were evolving into a protectiveness bordering on motherhood. Strange how people were, she thought as she mopped his brow dank with nightmares. You never knew where you were going next, just as you never knew where you had come from. What would she have thought, if twenty years ago, someone had suggested that she would be here, on the Algarve as Spring flooded in with its sex and almonds, loving and caring for a man of dusky complexion and forfeiting everything she had deemed precious in her previous existence? Never mind twenty years ago – what about three months ago? She had lost a man before but that been a hopeless, a desperate wrenching kind of love doomed to the eternity of death. This, on the other hand was a blossoming of heart's love deep in the sun of the morning.

On the fifth afternoon of the third week, Antonio awoke and was sane. He smiled weakly as she brought him a cup of tea.

Melanie Desmoulins

"Today, I must get up. I must begin to rebuild."

She kissed his forehead.

"...Don't be silly, you're far too weak to do anything of the sort."

He tried to get up and then fell back on his pillow.

"See – I told you. You should listen to me."

He took her hand.

"I don't know how to thank you..."

She pressed her finger to his dry lips.

He turned and sipped weakly from the cup.

"My hair is bleaching," she said, fingering the strands of gold as if she were a hippie.

"They say that you can tell who is of Algarve and who is not by whether their hair turns yellow or black in the sun."

"I must not be of this place, then."

"I didn't mean that."

She turned away from him, letting the hair fall across her face.

"No? It doesn't matter, anyway."

She paused.

"...Did Rachel's hair go black, or yellow?"

"Can't you tell?"

"I want you to tell me."

He sighed.

"Black," he said weakly. He was already exhausted.

"I just thought she might've dyed it, or something. I always knew she was of here. Meant to be here. For good or evil, better or worse..."

"I don't want to talk about her."

"Why not?"

"God! She was like that – always asking questions, always trying to get inside of everything. Sometimes, its better not to try. It's impossible, anyway. No-one can ever get inside anyone else. No-one can ever really belong to another person. Not really. Not ever. It's very English to try, though. I will never understand the English."

"Don't try."

"It's as if they cannot live in the countries in which they used to rule, so they come here and build their little private paradises in the sunshine where they play at being rich."

"But tourism has made this country."

"Made it, what?"

"I mean – before tourism, what was Portugal? Dictatorship and black skirts."

"We had our day."

They fell silent as the sky blew upwards in the wind.

"Did you know something?" he asked.

She looked quizzically at him.

"Did you know that England and Portugal have never gone to war? It's the only country which the English haven't fought against. Ever."

"Why is that, I wonder."

"Strategy."

"What?"

"Strategic necessity. Portugal was a thorn in the side of Spain and England was a boot in the face of Holland."

"...The ships?"

"That's it."

She pondered for a moment.

"Perhaps it was because we both face out across the open ocean. We're both flung out at the far ends of Europe. The great darkness sits upon our very shoulder."

The lid of the sea closed like the lid of a dead man and the squat sails of Navigator Henry trailed away over the world's edge.

"The greatest darkness is that within our soul."

The sun filtered through the blinds and fell in coils upon his face so that to her as she turned at the door, he resembled the divine fresco of a saint.

δδδδδδδδδδδδ

Rachel wandered from shadow to shadow, the whisper of a soul. Far to the north, in the still cool lands of Minho and Braganca, she scattered herself amongst dark forest and jagged mountain, amidst the sadness of empty bars and dank streams. And always, in the hushed silences of day and the clamouring inhumanity of night, there stole the white shade of Bartolomeo with his powders and potions, his boned fingers which had never been young. Rachel's dissolution became absolute in the dregs of this town. She wanted

Melanie Desmoulins

to splay herself in her million fragments all across the face of the blued sky, to let her soul soak into the stinging white wine, to dissolve at last in the gas of the sun.

She fragmented herself into five parts and each part courted one man. She prided herself on her ability to pull them like bulls toward her and then play with their desires coolly like the supreme matador of night. She enticed them by degrees into her madness. She drew their bulging, blue-veined cocks closer to one another and thence, to herself. She saw two paintings, dripping with oil and blood. In the first, the ring of toros ran around her, red with sweat and desire. They pulled the sinews of torn muscles from one another's loins, they crunched with the grind of white bone upon white bone. In the other, the flipside, she was the silent spider and they, the buzzing flies. By the time they saw one another, it would be too late, they would be beyond the realm of the mind and would be wallowing in the fetid reality of the body and its never-ending needs. And as the men, one by one, mounted and were mounted upon, one for each of her *toureiro*-spider's limbs, she felt their energy surge wildly into her flesh and her laughter bellowed across the frozen wastes like the howl of winter in the face of the silent sun. She smeared the men's pre-come all over her body. Her gleaming, worshipped body. She groaned with pleasure as she imagined the millions of tiny worms coursing over her skin. Her body convulsed with pleasure, each hole sucking on all the cocks at once. They came together, all five of them, and she smeared their come over her entire fucked frame. She ran it through her hair. Rubbed it into her gaping cunt. There was enough for her long, slim legs, right down to the painted toes. But still she was not satisfied. She pulled on the cocks again and again until they had given everything they had, and more. Until their vessels were dry. The men sank back from her. She laughed at them, the poor fool peasants who in that act had ceased to be human. She laughed at Antonio who once had been just a fool and who always would be love's victim. But most of all, she laughed at Lucy, the woman who lacked the spark of evil which could burn stone and lick heaven. From the depths of the pentagonal pit, Rachel roared with conquering glee at the certain destiny of the other woman whom she knew would rise like the saints, only to be cast down lower than the serpent. And when this happened, Rachel would sit on her lips and suck her vessel empty, and then she would smother her with her hot demon's wings.

eight

The man who deserves favours is, in the eyes of women, the one who is anxious to please them.

Lucy and Antonio built their lives together and three years passed in the building. Lucy's family accepted her choice without understanding it and Antonio's grandmother at last began to warm towards her.

A lie. A fiction.

Lucy's family did not accept her choice. Antonio's shrivelled grandmother remained cold as death towards her. The past slunk away to hide like Pelagio amongst the shrubbery and pale moonlight of the wilderness marches.

Antonio rebuilt the house. They made love in every room, every cupboard. And when they had grown bored with sex indoors, they would fuck in the garden, beneath bushes or against a tree-trunk.

Sex in the Dining-Room: A hard, wooden table. Lucy on her back, with her cunt dripping over the edge. Antonio standing.

Sex on the Stairs: The best place for hound-positions.

Sex in the Broom-Cupboard: The lack of oxygen was almost as good as a noose.

Sex in the Bedroom: They had a large, circular water-bed which doubled the effect of any movement.

Sex against the wall. Her back would emerge, torn to shreds against the whitewashed concrete. He would lick the blood off her and spoon his reddened tongue into her mouth.

Yet after three years of this heterosexual monogamy, boredom inevitably began to set in. Even the most exotic positions became routine. Neither of them would admit this, not even to themselves. But it was happening. One day, Antonio received a message:

I need to see you. Very important. The Café Segura. Three o'clock.
—R

He toyed with the piece of paper, which had arrived by courier. He wanted to crumple it up, toss it away, burn it as she had burned his home, his seven years of sanity. In his eye, he saw her crumpled, dying in the waste factory, being churned into chemical sludge and ending as nothing... Her with her big vulva, her tight anus. He read the message six times and with each reading, the thudding in his groin grew harder.

She was waiting at the café. With her big eyes and a long, evil-smelling cigarette. The smoke was familiar and in the swirling mist were images of wild days and wilder nights in the open, upon the broad mound of Alemtejo, the screams of animal pouring into the soft earth.

"Hello, Tony."

Her voice rasped upon a blade. Just like before, only harder, sharper. She was the only one who'd ever called him 'Tony'. He nodded, without nodding.

"Sit down."

She motioned to the chair opposite. He did not take his eyes off her. She was still slim, and was wearing the usual low-cut dress. It were as though it had been moulded onto her body. The soft touch of her velvet breasts in the moonlight. He looked away. He ordered a glass of *cerveja*.

"You've not changed."

"Why did you send for me?"

"I'm sorry about your house."

He flashed a look at her. Fire in his eyes.

"It was your house, too."

He paused.

"Was it you?"

She looked away.

"How's the wifey?"

"Don't call her that."

"Why not? Isn't that what she is? Isn't that why you followed her? Like a dog. I'm surprised you haven't ended up in England. Eating roast beef and Yorkshire pud..."

"I didn't come here to listen to this shit."

His voice was low and cold. The voice of a murderer.

"No."

She paused.

"I've been around... since we split. I kept remembering our first year together. Before Bartolomeo. I can't get it out of my mind."

"I am not interested."

He paused, then delivered the rapier.

"Before Bartolomeo, there was nothing."

He began to get up. His beer arrived. She spoke through ice.

"I have something that could damage you and your... paramour. And unless you listen, and listen now, I will use it."

He smirked.

"Don't talk rubbish..."

She flicked her cigarette up to shoulder-level. Like a snake.

"How can you be sure, Tony?"

"Don't call me that."

"Why? You used to like it. Before Bartolomeo."

He looked away, across the street. Tanned, long-limbed boys were following a set of pallid girls, newly-arrived. Both groups were almost naked.

"You must come with me."

"What!"

"Otherwise, you'll never see me again. And you'll never know what it is, I have. I might use it, any time. And you won't know."

She squinted at him and smiled. With her full, buttock lips.

"You came today. So there must be something left... between us."

"No. There is nothing. There never was, anything."

"You don't believe that! You don't believe your own lies, do you? Even if she does."

He was silent, but did not leave the café.

Two hours later, they were in Rachel's flat. It was dark, like the inside of a virgin. Rachel had never been a virgin. She was a kind of anti-virgin, a most immaculate conception. And from her legs, her long, limbed legs there flowed the sweet aroma of vice, the spider-rope of sex, the pull and stab of *touro* and *toureiro*. And though, in the pitch air he could no longer see her, yet he saw her more clearly than ever and with the despair of emptiness and joy, he saw that behind the years and the deceit and the hatred, his body belonged to her. For once baited and trapped, the bullfly could never escape. Never. He would submit to his disembowelling in a state of orgasm and would die, dreaming of maggot-gleam. With her long cat's teeth, she tore off his clothes. From somewhere, she produced a long, indigo feather and began tickling it unbearably along his skin. Wherever the feather went, it raised the surface of his skin in delicious mounds of desire. He moaned as she took him beyond the point of the death of the senses. Running her soft fingers over his body, she fell onto her knees and with fast flicks of her moist tongue, she licked at his bag. She worked her way along the creased skin, until the sack swelled to bursting-point. Each egg was the size of a lemon, but red with blood. His rod was already firm and throbbing in tune with the blood as it rushed through his ears. He threw his head back, and groaned. Slowly, inch by inch, she eased his velvet phallus-head onto her lips where she played with it for a while, teasing the purple mound with her tongue-tip. Then, millimetre by excruciating millimetre, she slid the organ deeper into the hot darkness of her mouth. She sucked him in with delicious little movements of her cheeks. Then she began to pull on the desperate cock using her throat muscles. Gently at first, then more vigorously. His hands gripped her by the shoulders, digging the nails deep into her skin. His feet slapped quickly apart. He took care not to allow the centre of his body to shift, so much so did he need the rough pull of her palate. His penis was an umbilical cord leading to the red-hot hard softness of her mouth. And from the dark cavern of words and delicious pressures, there came the exquisite heaven of Hell. His whole length was in her now, right up to the very root, right down to his beginnings. He could feel her throat gag on his swollen flesh. And with each downward gag-suck, the pleasure grew more and more intense, until his series of broken moans became a low-pitched growl which went on, no matter whether he was breathing in, or out. She pulled him out and the pain grew to be unbearable. She slid down his throat with the ease of warm brandy.

Melanie Desmoulins

With her hot, rough-skinned tongue, she ladled his eggs almost painfully, threatening all the while to crush them and produce unbearable agony which would surge up his loins and finish him forever. He knew he was at her mercy. He knew he had always been her slave and nothing more. If she had ordered him at that moment, to squeeze a shit from her anus into his open mouth, he would gladly have done it. If she had demanded that he throw Lucy down into the ocean and throttle her there with the cold sardine waves, his hand would have been the first upon her throat. If she had commanded him to become the serf of her pentagonal bulls and to be rodded through by each of them in turn while she stamped her foot upon his head, he would have been the first to flare his anus. Glistening moist pink open in the centre of the pentangle. He would have worshipped any number of hoary Satans, have burned foetuses alive on dung pyres while big dogs mounted women and men spermed asses. As she tasted the pungency of his pre-come on her palate, she flung a cord around his neck and pulled the ends tightly. His breathing, already issuing in rapid, panting succession, in and out, in and out, now became irregular and tortured. A pain greater than life throbbed in his temples. His eyes grew from black to star-grey and a line of sweet sweat began to flow from his opened anus. Rachel was empress of his dying brain. She sat upon a chariot pulled by his man-horse body. Deep, bleeding welts slashed across his delicate buttocks as she drove him mercilessly towards the darkness of oblivion. With a gold sceptre, she impaled him from behind, roaring all the while with the laughter of triumph. The victory-scream of serf over master, of pig over farmer, of woman over man. As the pulsing in his head slowed, his breath stopped and he became rigid, a statue cast in metal. He felt himself lift up and soar above the room. Above the sweating, fellating beast, in the darkness of lust he rose. Below him, were all beings joined to one another in circles of light. He saw Lucy – yes, Lucy with her long, creamy legs and her erotic, painted toes. Even she was joined to the great wifemother beast at the heart of the spiralling web. The gaping wound no longer had a name, for it had dispersed itself throughout the quivering flesh of female and non-female. It ran on taut wires of kill, outward to the very edge of the light. With one enormous sucking motion which drew his whole body towards her mouth, she pulled him to the cliff-edge. Beyond, lay nothing but darkness. In that moment of no oxygen, his heart quivered on the brink of emptiness. She released the cord and he poured down her throat. He had turned to liquid, to the silken stickiness of sin. He slumped down, still inside her, and she held the liquid to her body.

In that moment, she knew she had won.

Lucy awoke with a start. She was drowning. For a moment, she wondered whether she were still dreaming but then she realised it was sweat, and not seawater which covered her pale belly. The space beside her, was a space. Empty and cold. She got up and swung open the window. The night was smothered in sweat. She drew on the air like it was a cigarette but all she got was the stench of humanity, stretching all the way to the edge of the ocean. The sea where she had just drowned. She tasted its salt limbs, its bestial breath, the darkness of its murder. Then she remembered she'd chucked it years earlier. Fags. Going back into the room, she picked up a bottle of Medronho and took a large swig. She swallowed hard. Her chest began to explode, slowly. She spluttered and coughed and smashed the bottle down. A thin stream of colourless fluid slid like dead men's sperm from its side. She went back to bed and closed her eyes.

δδδδδδδδδδδδ

With the flats of both palms upon her shoulders, he threw her down on all fours. Working all the while in the small, moist triangle of flesh which sat just below her pubes, using his other hand he tickled around the crumpled skin of her arsehole. Then, gradually he edged his index finger in. The shameless pout of her anus welcomed him with a slimy stream of mucous. She felt her insides open up. He began moving in and out. She opened her mouth, and her shithole widened. Suddenly, there were two fingers inside her. Her clit was running with the sap of her sex. She knew she was rising and falling like the waves of the sea. A delicious, quivering feeling clawed its way all over her body, from her swollen button outwards and with a roar, she climaxed. He would not stop, and she came again. And again. Wave upon wave upon wave.

δδδδδδδδδδδδ

Melanie Desmoulins

She was in the middle of a pentagon of male lust. One man was in her vagina, another had rammed into her rectum while a third and fourth were swollen and moist in the palms of her clenched fists. She was mare-panting. Suddenly, a man whose face she could not see because she was impaled belly-down on the first man's rearing phallus, came up and jerked her head upwards. With a single motion, he shoved his rough member into her mouth. She tasted its salt. It was the roller of the sea, it was the unseen creature which lurked blindly on the black floor of the ocean, it was the madness that throbbed in the belly of every angel, before it fell. Every thrust of the man's haunches made her gag. She wanted to vomit but the was unable to. She was being shoved in all directions by the five swollen beasts.

She was a hog bitch, being rutted for the first time. A pig virgin, falling into the abyss. As the animals coursed into her body, she felt herself dissolve into blackness. On the face of the dark, she saw his face. His five face.

His children tasted of the ocean.

δδδδδδδδδδδδδ

She was lying in the dark.

A gentle tickling around her lips, her arsehole, her clit caused her to awaken. The fingers were thin, muscular, experienced. They moved inside her anus and her vagina at the same time while still roving over her tiny, throbbing phallus. She began to make pig-sounds, her pink flesh quivering with delight. The fingers made her come twice in thirty seconds. After her second climax, she felt the hard nipples of a woman push into her back and the hot breath of Medronho flared in her nostrils.

"Bitch. Hog-bitch. I've got him. He's mine. I'll never let him go."

Lucy awoke.

She was sodden.

The space between bits of her shouted in a streaming wind.

The space beside her was empty.

nine

She threw herself upon him, took his member between her hands and began to look at it. She was astonished at its size, strength and firmness, and cried, "Here we have the ruin of all women and the cause of many troubles!"

She knew what it was like to be invisible. She knew Antonio no longer looked at her when he fucked her. He closed his eyes and fucked someone else. She took to following him at night. She saw them meet, kiss, grope and then she went with them into a room high up in a deserted building. Through a crack in the wall, she watched them as they screwed like dogs on an old mattress on the bare floor. And as she watched, she felt the pull of gravity upon her hand. She tore at her clothes and made herself one with the screaming couple. She knew she should have hated him, should have killed them both where they lay, open-legged. But she didn't. She wanted them. Both. One day, she could bear it no longer, and she burst in on them as they lay together, totally naked. Rachel looked up at her, and smiled.

"I knew you would come." Her voice was red velvet. It smelled of her cunt.

Lucy took hold of Antonio and tore him out of the whore's hole, out from the vice of her long legs. Placing herself astride him, she forced his already moist member into herself and began to move up and down upon the loose skin. Rachel lit a cigarette and watched as they came together. Then Lucy watched as Rachel had her turn with him. But just as he was about to climax, Lucy ran across the room and clutching Rachel by her breasts, she tore her off the straining male below. She tore at her skin, kicking, biting, gobbing.

Melanie Desmoulins

She pulled her hair out by the roots. As the hot liquid of love poured from Antonio's open-mouthed organ, the two women wrestled madly with each other, drawing blood from the weals on their backs. Their wet cunts kissed, the tiny phalluses rubbing up against each other. Finally, insanely, screaming in tandem they drove their tongues into each other's cavernous openings. They were two glorious white bodies, one upon the other, identical like gods and they had no need of the man. The weaker sex. The prick sex. Their caverns were larger than any prick could ever imagine. Rachel relaxed, and a stream of burning, yellow urine flooded over Lucy's breasts. The nipples tautened. They both lapped at the slithering fluid, as dogs might.

"My dog," Rachel purred, as Lucy bit into the leaves of her cunt.

"My bitch," she murmured, breathlessly.

"I've always wanted you, you blonde bombshell. Ever since I set eyes upon you."

"I've always known you, you dark whore. You black bitch." Rachel groaned in agony. Lucy could not stop.

"I want to inflict pain on you. I want to feel you squirm. I want you to teeter on the edge of insanity. I want to push you over the edge."

She paused. The two women were breathless, panting like beasts.

"I want to kill you, and to watch you die. And then I want to die, myself, and to feel my own death. That would be the ultimate climax."

Then Lucy lay on top of her as a man might, in a kind of lesbian missionary position. She laughed at the thought, throwing her head back in a thrust of triumph. She bit into the other woman's nipples without mercy, but this was just what Rachel wanted, and she begged her fuck-mate for more pain, more pain, more pain. The blood ran down the sides of her trembling body, and still she pleaded for more. A hot flow of urine gushed out from between her thighs and mixed with the blood in strange, curving rivulets. In the wet grind of bone upon bone, in the meeting of bulbous, swollen lips, in the horror of unity was their anger sated. The two women knew that they had never really had any need of the man, pathetic beast that he was. They needed only each other. The whole thing had been an act. The romance, the anger, the suicide attempt. It had all been necessary to pull Lucy out of her shell. The shell of twenty-five years of marriage. The suffocating chrysalis of motherhood and widowhood. He had been merely a conduit, a prick, a cock, on the way from one woman to another. *Ride a cock-horse to Banbury Cross.* Fuck him, and fuck his Cross. He would fade out of the picture as surely as the dinosaurs had vanished from the newly-fecund earth. The meek would inherit it, alright. But the women would not be meek. They would be screaming in orgasmic splendour. One cunt upon one cunt. One clit upon one clit. Forever.

At the end of it all, the three figures lay side-by-side, puffing on joints. Lucy wondered what her daughter would have thought of all this. And the people in the office? She was unable to control a laugh from escaping her thickened, bruised lips. She didn't care. For the first time in her life, she was enjoying herself. For the first time ever, she was no longer somebody's wife, someone's mother, some firm's tool (she laughed again). She was herself, stripped to the bone. She was taking what she wanted, and it felt good. It felt like she was being born. Life began here. There was no longer any jealousy. Rachel had felt jealousy – that was why she had burned Antonio's house down – but now she too, had come beyond that. Lucy felt they were reaching peaks which society, religion, morals prevented people from climbing. Maybe for most people, they were necessary evils, to save men and women from glancing at things which they would be unable to handle, which might destroy them or send them beyond the gates of madness. And there were times when Lucy had felt close to destruction. But she knew she was too strong for that. Rachel had drink and drugs. Lucy had her inner strength. She would survive.

ठठठठठठठठठठठ

Bit by bit, Antonio faded more and more into a kind of background. He became an object which the two women might use in order to arouse themselves when they grew bored. Mostly, Lucy and Rachel enjoyed exploring one another. There was so much more in a woman's love. They knew best how to give pleasure to each other. It was so much deeper. To feel the contours of your own body heave and thrust beneath the softness of your own palm. The glow of the tribad. The wondrous bud of life, that which men down the prick-filled ages had tried to hide, curtail, maim, deny. A touch whose beauty lay in its subtlety. Something that could never be understood by men. The enigmatic smile of a woman's lips, the time between the waves of her desire, the knowledge of snake-thrusts one into the next, to which only the female mouth could aspire. The love of woman for woman. While the lust between woman and man is in the thrill of unfamiliarity, of opposites, the bond between two women is akin to that of gazing endlessly into a mirror. It was a kind of narcissism. In Rachel, Lucy saw herself, and through her dissolution she perceived her own decay. In Rachel, she saw that the end was always beyond where it had been, a moment earlier. It always eluded. The passion, as they said, was in the chase. And she loved to love the monster that was herself. She noticed that Rachel had begun to adopt some of her mannerisms and by the same token, Lucy began to try some of the potions and powders which the other woman possessed, procured no doubt from that strange slice of a man who drifted around at night, dressed all in white. A needle in her vein would give her entire body a climax which she had not thought possible. Every inch of her skin would rise into orgasm all at once so that she would want to die quickly. She felt her heart stop and in the time of death's embrace, she would feel Rachel, even if she were not there. She fitted exactly into Rachel's contours, into the smiling body of the other woman. Together, they were becoming a great, fat mother-goddess. The fatter, the better. By gradual degrees, she felt herself sinking into Rachel's very soul, so that she began to understand the other woman perfectly. This is what it must have like in the beginning, this is what it had been like in the cold ocean, in the deep dark forest, in the relentless boil of volcano slime.

"I never thought I would be a lesbian," she said, one afternoon as they rose from their bed.

Rachel smiled. Lucy could see this, even though the figure had her back turned towards her and was standing in the window, framed in light and wood like a renegade saint. An angel, long fallen. Her buttocks were bulbous. Deliciously obscene. Lucy could see her long, whore's nipples reflected in the window. She felt the beginnings of desire rise in her. A tweaking of her heart.

"Those are just words, given by idiots. The thing is,

everything in the world – everything – is there for a reason. If women weren't meant to be attracted to each other, then it simply wouldn't be. There's nothing wrong in it. There never has been."

"What about murder?"

Rachel spun round. Her pubic hair had a tinge of red amidst the black. Or maybe it was the setting sun.

"What about it?"

"If everything which is, is right then does that mean that killing someone – or killing yourself – is right, too?"

"You should stop thinking in terms of 'right and wrong'. Murder is just killing and killing is how nature eats. Without killing, there is no life. Without death, there is no birth."

"I like pricks. Long, hard, blue-veined cock-a-doodle-doos begging you to take them in out of the cold. I like the way they slowly sag in my mouth after they've come. Or the way their tiny mouth opens deep inside me and releases its hot packet. The stiffness of just before. Like a stick that's about to snap. I want to see it snap and the blue blood come gushing from every vein. I want to feel the blood mix with the spunk in my womb. I want to suck the broken snake into my body, so that it might become mine. And then I, too would be able to feel what a man feels with his long cock. I too would be able to grow stiff and to spurt all over the place within thirty seconds of touching myself."

"But it's over too quickly with them, don't you think? I mean, we can come and come for hours-on-end. We can take twenty men and come three times with each of them – all on one night – but try that with one of them, and they'd be dead. Knackered!"

Lucy laughed. It was the laugh of the whore. Rachel grew coy.

"But then, I've had tons of men. You've only had two."

She puffed on a joint as she mouthed this. The smoke in her face made Lucy want to cough, but she held her breath so she wouldn't.

"So have I."

Rachel looked puzzled.

Lucy remembered the whore, the priest, the alley-woman, the boulder-man, the tramp. She'd been them all. She'd had them all. She felt the lust of vampires. Insatiable. Never-ending. A snake within her.

Melanie Desmoulins

The snake smiled.

She rolled another thread of white and placing the end of the paper in her nostril, she inhaled sharply. A rush of snakes sliced through her body. Every time was more bloody than the next, every minute worse and better. Her breaths came in short bursts, as though time had pulled them taut.

I am the fille de joie
I am the temptress, the scarlet bitch, the fornicatress
I am the Messalina, the paramour, the leman
I am the harlot, the hussy, the hetaera
I am the cocotte, the lorrette, the poule
I am Paphian
I am Cyprian
I am Aspasia
I am woman
She inhaled again
Fuck Boss
Fuck Mother
Fuck Father
Fuck Peter
Fuck Jane
O shit
Fuck the One.

"I can fuck like a man," Rachel began.

She proceeded to stuff a big black imitation penis between her lips and up her cunt. But her bed-mate grabbed the long phallus from her.

"My turn to be a man," Lucy urged. She was man, and woman, and everything in between and beyond.

Rachel smiled, and joined her and together, they *did* fuck the One.

ẟẟẟẟẟẟẟẟẟẟẟẟ

One night, she was lying alone in bed beneath a voilé sheet, when a large, black dog entered the room. The dog paused at the door, its red gob panting. Its nostrils flared and snorted obscenely and its soft tongue stuck out like a limp phallus. Slowly, she turned over and as she did so, she felt the thin sheet slide deliciously off her back. She raised herself up on all fours. She heard the pad-pad of the beast as it came towards her. She felt the gentleness of its claws as it mounted her soft, white back. Its hot, wet breath warmed her skin, sending ripples up and down her body. The dog was heavy and the weight of its body forced her rear quarters down, so that she was on hands and knees. The long, course tongue lapped her back, her shoulders, the lips of her vulva, the skin of her arsehole. Then suddenly she felt a searing pain as the beast pushed inside her. She screamed, while from the dog, there issued a low growl. Its voice was deep, powerful. The rod within her was bone-hard. It moved faster and more surely than any man's ever had. She felt the dog's jaws clamp gently around her left shoulder. Her nipples were pointed, taut as beads. Within seconds, the dog had come in her body. She wondered whether she would give birth to a race of dogmen who would have pricks of bone and tongues of poetry. She felt the beast's sperm race towards her womb in anticipation of their conquest. The dog pulled out. The withdrawal was excruciating, callous, delicious. When she turned around, the dog had gone.

Next morning, she mentioned the incident to Rachel when she returned loaded with shopping-bags. Rachel laughed and told her that it was only Demonio come to visit all women who had freed themselves of lies, and that she should welcome him and his bony desire. And night after night, Demonio would come and impale her and every time, he would take on a different form. First a dog, then a bull, then a horse and then a lion. Once, he came as a serpent and became lost inside her. Another time, she became a great faecolith vulva awaiting the return of its twin sister. Waiting with dripping clitoris for the end of time, the ultimate, tearing orgasmic crescendo, the last rabid yell of the dog-shit burning on the deserted pavement of the sludge-suckers. From every turgid sweat-gland of her slimy, anti-phallic dream, Lucy spouted excreta; final waste which she then ate in a hemibalismic orgy of satiation. The faeces ran through her smooth, snake gut like the phallus of a gigolo immersed in the semen of a thousand nights, only to emerge from the gaping grimace of her labial slit, a fully-fledged woman, limbs-and-all. Lucy recognised her daughter and then, as the skin of the tanned sulphurous entity slipped off its poor, naked skeleton, she saw

Melanie Desmoulins

herself. Her worried, suburban self. Fuckless. Dry. *Never again!* She
screamed at the top of her anus. And she invited all of the demons
of the hot, deserted Manchas to come and screw her through every
sebaceous opening in her multi-pored corpus. They joined together
and grew into the longest penis known to woman and fucked her
with the relish of a slave. Then Lucy became a thousand penis-heads
and burned red into the anuses of the demons, sending them back
to Hell where they would fuck only the frozen carcasses of priests.
Most affectionately, Demonio took out a stick of bright red lipstick
and, using his sharp dog's teeth, he carved it into the shape of a
long, mutant phallus. He parted her already-soaking thighs and
smeared her anus, her vulva and the sensitive bit in between with
the thick, oily lip-smegma. He then proceeded to impale her with
the same, hellish instrument, causing orgasm upon orgasm, mounting
one another like wild dogs knowing no sex, no natural boundaries.
The living raced with the dead, and the non-living bred schools of
doomed babies from within the cathedral of her vagina. This was
reality. Everything else – her past life, the morals she had been
taught, the restrictions of the fiancé and the guilt of the widow – all
this, was illusion. Every cell in her body needed sex, and she was
ready to obtain it, again and again and again. Even beyond death's
fake orifice. She wished now that she had screwed Peter on his
death-bed, that she had necrophallised his scrotum as it decomposed
into mush. She had felt like it at the time. Somewhere, deep in the
soul of her solar plexus, she had desired, not his prattling, groaning
sick life, but his monster-weaning death-rattle in her throat. Close to
the heaven of faecal decomposition, Lucy had scented immortality.
And she liked the smell. She wondered what all the fuss had been
about – Antonio's guilt, Rachel's jealousy, her own moralizing, their
silly little romance – when it had all been so simple, all along. They
had been picked, right from that first day on the verandah. From
before that. Perhaps they had all been chosen, before they had even
existed in the world of flesh and sex, before even they had existed
on the dry page of birth. Everything else had been a game. Antonio
was weak. Men were weak. He had strayed from the path. It wasn't
the albino Rachel had met that scorching day up on the hill. It was
Antonio. She had tried to pull him back into the fold. Rachel and
Antonio had played with each other's emotions, over the years, until
there was nothing left. Only the bare-backed beast of sex in the dirt

of their souls. There lay truth. Naked truth. And from this void, would they perceive of their true selves. Without morals, without chains, free as fish in the endless blue. But Rachel had become strung up on booze and dope, while Antonio like most men, confused sex with romance. And now Lucy was part of their game. Now she had partaken of the cup of lust and dissolved herself in its fire. And now, like the phoenix was she reborn and would never be the same again. Outwardly, she maintained appearances, wrote to her daughter, went shopping, swam in the sea. After a time, she found she no longer needed drugs or booze. Words gradually fell away and became redundant. But she found she could read the minds of men and dogs and could make both howl at the moon in desire of her. This was the way it had been, in the oldest of days when woman had ruled all. She was no longer certain which was real, that or this. What did it matter, anyway? They would go off into the mountains where the waters were of magical silver. In a hill forest where, many centuries earlier, heretic monks had consorted with renegade nuns and ceremonially orgied beneath a moon full with the glow of spunk-worms, the three of them would disperse themselves among the beasts and the vermin. Rachel was too immersed in the blindness of stimulation, Antonio couldn't see beyond the end of his prick. But she knew there was more. She had been through romance with a man and now through Rachel had she dug herself out of the living grave of womanhood. She knew, as she lay with her dog-calloused back upon the coarse lumps of virginal soil that one day the great god of the earth, the lewd goatgod, the bullheaded king of fertility would come with his two-foot phallus and offer her the joy of immolation. It would be the last moment of her life and the most glorious. To return from whence she had arisen. To be One with the Lord Of The Earth. To be the earth.

Melanie Desmoulins

ten

Her thirst for coition is written between her eyes.

The speed-boat was long and sleek and white and it shone like the penis of a Swede in the Portuguese sun. Antonio owned the craft and had steered it far out to sea, where they could only just make out the thin line of land to their backs. He switched off the engine and opened a bottle of white wine. They drank long and deep, straight from the bottle's opened mouth. The wine was strong. Lucy felt her head begin to swim. Rachel was used to much, much more and drank as though it was her last. At length, her eyes began to glaze over as Lucy felt her own had already done. She moved over to where Lucy was sitting.

"Let's do it here."

"What – in the middle of the ocean?"

"Why not? What better place could there be? No-one about, for miles. A clear view. Heaven on the water."

The two women wore only bikinis. With her wine'd hands, Rachel began to caress her body. Lucy closed her eyes. It felt good. The sun upon her brow, the water running a mile beneath her, the breeze empty of everything. Empty of guilt. She felt her bra ease off her breasts. A warm feeling enveloped them as the sun spread itself all over the pale skin.

"You should bathe topless more often," Rachel mouthed in her ear, "You have lovely breasts."

"We'll bathe together. Nude."

"Yes, yes, yes..."

The soft curves of the other woman's body moved upon her own, the small of her pelvis, the firm bones of her knees, the warm splay of her feet. Rachel's arms played down her back, exciting tingles of joy to run in shoals up and down her skin. The vine of her lips teased at Lucy's. First one, then the other. Then her tongue slithered its way into her mouth, lapping greedily at her own, searching for the perfect twine. Their tongues were tropical branches, twirling without end, fronds sinuous and livid each trying to outdo the other in a grand imitation of the snake. Rachel was also naked and she felt the grind of her pelvic bone against her own. The perfection of woman was complete. Whole like the earth, like the sea. No edges. A circle of flesh. Man had only been created as some kind of mirror, so that perfection might know itself by the presence of imperfection. The glass mirror could only be seen by the blemish on its surface. Once the blemish had been wiped off, perfection would be regained. The woman's fingers were working between her legs, rubbing slowly, rolling it beneath the tips. Lucy moaned. The boat bobbed up and down on the gentle waves, and Lucy felt as though her feet were no longer on the ground. Her back was pressed against the wooden hull of the vessel. The gleaming sides pulled taut like skin over the wood. Rachel grabbed her long, golden hair and tugged her head backwards, so that she had to splay her feet in order to keep her balance. The wetness slid from under her. Her breath was coming in short gasps. She felt the pressure of something cold and smooth press against the lips between her thighs. She opened her eyes.

"Don't worry. You'll like it," Rachel whispered in her ear.

Gently, excruciatingly slowly, Rachel eased the smooth metal dome into her vagina. She gripped the woman's slightly rounded shoulders and dug her long, painted nails into the skin. She sensed the quiver of pain which coursed through her lover's body and she drew out the pain in trails along her back. There was the rip of penetration through the jealous sphincter of her anus. This was different from the black phallus which they had tried before. Sleeker. Harder. Better.

"Tear me! Tear me to shreds!" Rachel whispered. Her breath was hotter than the sun upon Lucy's neck. She pushed the douche in as far as it would go.

"God, your cunt's so long..."

"My cunt goes on forever."

Rachel began working the silver penis in and out, slowly at

Melanie Desmoulins

first but then with more insistence. Involuntarily, Lucy legs splayed out further. The boat moved in glorious circles upon the waves, up and down and from side to side and the douche moved with the vessel. Flames began to course up from her clit and drew her body taut like a sail in the wind.

"Yes, yes, yes, yes, yes... more, more, more, more, more..." she cried.

"I want this to last forever," Rachel whispered in her voice of red-hot coals.

"Forever."

Lucy roared as she had never roared before as she came to climax. It seemed to go on for minutes. Her cries flew on feathers across the sea's belly and made the old waves churn with delight. When she came round, she realised she had defaecated onto the deck.

Rachel began to move the phallus again, but Lucy pulled it out, whispering,

"My turn to be a man."

"You always say that."

"I know. I like saying it."

Rachel lay luxuriantly back against the side of the boat, and closed her eyes. She murmured seductively through her pouted lips.

"I want you, you fucking blonde bombshell. I want to rip out your blonde pubic hair with my teeth, I want to possess your body here, on this boat. I want your fucking cunt to slide inside me and take me on the floor. I want to feel your golden hair all over my skin, my breasts, my nipples, my belly. I need you."

Her eyes opened and her voice grated like that of harridan.

"I need you!"

Lucy greased the tower with lubricant, delicious, oily lubricant, and slid it between her own swollen, desirous outer lips covered as they were in shining, blonde fur, and slowly, she pushed it further in. It had four prongs - one for each woman's vagina and one for the twin shitholes. It seemed odd, to have this big long silver duplex rod sticking out from between her legs. She began to giggle. Easing her thing into Rachel's waiting cunt-and-rear, she played for a while around the clit and the anal margin, both women giggling all the while like schoolgirls. The stubborn stick found its way up Rachel's twin caverns and Lucy began to move it in and out, in and out. Each thrust fired an electric pressure through her own clit, every pull threatened to suck her own rectum inside-out. It was a quadruplet cock, one end inside Rachel, the other end within her. Like a church with four spires. The female beasts were like sexual Siamese twins. They were the two ends of the same snake. Both were being fucked by the same cock, at the same time. Each was a woman, and yet both were men. The quadruple buggery. The boat was a Sodom of fours. Lucy felt the triumph of insulting nature. Of defying God.

"Take me! Take me! Take my soul!" both beasts yelled in unison, as the sun's rays caught the metal surface of the phallus held between their lips. Lucy felt the rabid hot ripples of having a woman's body next to hers, her spine arched taut as she felt the age-old desire of cunt for cunt. Pure, virgin, chaste desire. Love me, love me, love me!! the voice inside her head yelled, Please, please, please!!!

There was no comparison. None. She slithered up the mountain of Hell and it felt bloody good.

Fucking good.

Give me more! More!

Rachel, experienced hooker that she was, gave her more.

Lick my tits. Now!

Rachel drew her long, snake's tongue over Lucy's bursting nipples.

Lick my lips with your lips

The black-haired bitch pouted in Lucy's groin. Lip upon lip upon lip. Clit-lick Clit-lick Clit-lick Clit-lick

Yes! Yes! Yes! Yes! Yes!

Rachel yanked the silver rod

Out

O God

Delicious yank

Out

Out

Out

Her fucking tongue was on Lucy's golden cunt.

Flicking in and out

Her burning breath

Snake

Melanie Desmoulins

Tongue
Snake
Tongue
In
And
Out
In
And
Out
In
And
Out
O God O God O God O God O God O God
Yes Yes Yes Yes Yes Yes Yes Yes Yes Yes Yes

The climax, when it came, was the final victory of the incubi over the angels. The slimy, gleaming rod was the reborn power of the serpent.

Before she opened her eyes again, she felt a suddenly wrench of her shoulders. Antonio grabbed Rachel by the arms and flung her aside. She fell backwards onto the wooden deck. He was utterly naked and his phallus was bulging as she had never seen it bulge. It was crimson and wet at the tip, and throbbed up and down as the blood of desire coursed through its shaft. There was madness in his gaze. The pupils had opened up beyond imagining, making his eyes completely black. Without speaking, he roughly turned her around and grabbing the douche which was still in her body, he began working it. With his other hand, he made circles around her buttocks, drawing them in lines, drawing the lines in and in, so that at last he was teasing at the rumpled skin around her arsehole. She felt the muscles around her anus go slack and open, and a warm slime slipped out from the pouting flower mouth. He bit the nape of her neck. He was silent. Only the harsh rasp of his breath on her soft skin and the desperate movements of the joints in his pelvis around her gaping shit-hole revealed the urgency of his desire. He was the hunter, he was the ravaging horde-beast, the seed of Satan's prick and he had come to claim that which was his. She felt the ripple of defeat slither through her pelvis. There was joy in being taken like a slave, a concubine, an object. She wanted him to slap her. He slapped her. Hard. She wanted him to slap her again. He slapped her again. Harder. He pulled back her hair and bit her lower lip till it bled. He licked the blood onto her nostrils. The stink of her own heart's blood sent her body into a rapture she had never before endured. Her heart was beating so hard, she knew it must burst. Her arsehole was open to the breeze, and he filled it. First with his thumb, then with each of his fingers in turn. He drew them along the coarse walls of her gut, wiggling them like the bodies of tiny serpents. It were as if she were being fucked by ten different snakes. She cried out. A harsh, tearing, joyous scream that sliced through the water and was answered by copulating dolphins far below. Withdrawing his last, shit-stained finger, he thrust his great, bone-hard phallus into her body. She felt his seed-swelled sack balloon up against the ticklish area between her buttocks and she knew that they would burst unless her beast was conquered soon. Romance had evaporated and in its place had sprung the animal of the earth, the Lord Of Damnation, the great temptation of the flesh. The truth. The mindless truth. And she loved it. The roar of engines thundered from beneath her. Rachel had started the boat up. She caught a glimpse of the naked woman, steering the craft like some demented siren through the waves. Very quickly, the vessel got up speed, and the spray splashed past the two copulating figures, streaking them with ice-cool lick of its foam. Lucy felt the twin phalluses in the warmth of her flesh grow and swell. This would be a double climax. She let her head fall to the side, its golden mantle sodden with sea-spray. Rachel had left the wheel. There was no-one steering. The boat was completely out of control. It swerved this way and that, a crazed animal in the midst of three crazed animals. Naked in their splendour. Rachel was tonguing the man's arsehole, the pungent taste of shit making her want to vomit. She thrust her tongue in deeper, in and out, in and out, massaging the bulge that lay at the far end of the soft cavern. She wanted to vomit into his arse, to turn everything upside-down, to fuck with her stomach. The three of them moved upon the careering ship as the burning ball of fire in the sky tore their skins in bloody streaks, as the salt of the sea flowed mercilessly into their wounds, gnawing at their insides as only the truly mindless can.

As the man's seed exploded into her behind, his shit slipped out in hot sludges into Rachel's waiting mouth. Lucy reached up to the sky and fell deep into the ocean as the twin mouths of her

Melanie Desmoulins

creation screamed with the joy of death. The track of the ship cut across the sea in twisting coils which drew back upon themselves as if trying to perfect the curve of a snake upon water.

ẟẟẟẟẟẟẟẟẟẟẟẟ

The ropes were strong and white. They were slung between the thick rafters in great loops. Seven loops.

Antonio's body hung suspended between two of the ropes, one, around his wrists, the other wrapped tightly around his ankles. He was totally naked in the murky light. There were no windows and the walls were black, but a glow must have been coming from somewhere, because his body seemed almost incandescent. His long organ drooped like a sad, blind worm from between his thighs. Six other men lay suspended from the rafters in like fashion. The seven formed a ring around the room, a kind of phallic chandelier. Lucy and Rachel entered the room. They, too were naked, and each carried a bundle in her hand. Lucy unfurled her bundle. A long, sleek black whip glinted in the strange half-light. Rachel did the same. They began to stroll around the room, drawing the whips slowly across the nipples of each man. Within seconds, the phalluses had stiffened. The two women now circled more quickly, stroking each of the cocks in turn and squeezing the balls till they swelled like the throats of frogs. Uncoiling her lash to its full, glorious length, Lucy drew it back and let it fly against Antonio's skin. He groaned with pain. She whipped him again, and again, drawing out great weals across his helpless body. All this time, his organ was lengthening and hardening. With each lash, the thing throbbed and grew. His eyes were closed. Blood dripped onto the stone floor. Rachel had started on the another of the men. One by one, the women lashed all seven of the groaning, squealing creatures. Then, throwing aside their whips, they took the cocks into their mouths and began to suck, hard. They moved round the circle like crazed bell-ringers, mouthing the phalluses till the bodies to which they belonged screamed out for release. As the fat snakes were on the verge of spurting out their contents, the women withdrew their lips and began to touch each other. They lay down on the cold floor and entwined their limbs. They mouthed each other's cunts and ground together the bones of their groins. Delicious grinding. Maddening

---

friction. Lucy yelled out.

"Fuck me fuck me fuck me fuck me fuck me fuck me !!!"

A two-backed beast, the women slowly mounted to orgasm, and as the flecks of light seared through her body, Lucy roared with abandon. As she came, she felt the hot spunk of seven cocks pour down onto her back. The silver fire mingled with the sweat of her muscles, and before the first climax was over, she had come again. Rachel rammed a black phallus between her buttocks, and began working her sphincter. She had shoved the base of the stiff cock into her vagina and was bumming Lucy as a man would. Everything gaped. Searing pain. Bloody joy. Rachel was in. With each thrust of the hard cock, a wave of pain and delight rippled through her body. The feel of a man-woman fucking her made her arch her back to meet the nipples of the strange beast.

"More! More!" she moaned.

And Rachel gave her more. Both women were now delirious and screamed, grunted and sighed with equal fervour. The rods above them had grown stiff again, and the men twisted and coiled in their fetters. They begged the women for release. Not release from the ropes, but sexual release. That, or death.

Lucy felt mounting waves draw through her belly. They washed over her brain and spread out to the tips of her fingers. She tore the nails through the other woman's nipples.

"Yes.! Yes! Hurt me! Tear me!" Rachel whispered.

Her own nipples had swelled and were now cherry-hard. Her neck arched. Rachel took hold of both whips and began to thrash her all over. The climaxes came for hours. The women were awash with the secretions of their own bodies, the sticky spunk of the men, and the blood of tearing, whipping and biting. The glorious whore-bitches writhed about on the slippery floor, swallowing up as much of the stuff as they could, and then gobbing it into each others' mouths. With their long, flicking tongues.

Lucy's thoughts flowed with the urine
Snake
Fuck
Me
Till
I

Melanie Desmoulins

Am
Like
You
Snake
Fuck
Me
Till
I
Am
You
Yes
Yes
Yes
Yes
Yes

jataveshtitaka

Orestes:	*Better be silent. Someone inside might hear you.*
Elektra:	*Ho, but I'm not afraid of them!*
	By the virgin Artemis, no, not afraid
	Of a houseful of good-for-nothings,
	Women!
Orestes:	*Remember, women are sometimes warriors too.*
	You have good reason to know it.

Long tongue licks at red petals
Long tongue creams around edges of red petals
Red petals weep
Hot tears
Sticky
Long tongue thrusts between red petals
Into cave of flower
Hard body follows behind long tongue
Coarse
Cold
Ancient
Hard body twists into a ball
Rims
Cave of flower
Bursts
Through walls
Sucks
Blood of flower
Flower dies
Joyous

Melanie Desmoulins

Lucy poured the violaceous cocktail into a long-stemmed glass and handed it to her daughter. The younger woman accepted it with some reluctance – partly because she had come down to this hot Portuguese fag-end cove, not to indulge in the social grace of drinking, but to argue, to get her mother to see sense at last, to take her away from this strange country, these unfamiliar people who it seemed had bewitched her – and partly because she recognised something mysteriously alien yet familiar in the smile of the woman whose fanny had spewed her out no different than a blob of shit. Keen to get the damn niceties over with, the blonde, long-haired bitch gobbed the rich concoction down her throat with the nonchalance of a whore at her prime. She licked her lips and tossed the glass aside. It hit a rock and smashed into a thousand pieces. Each piece of silver sand reflected the entire scene within the cove through the red gash of viscous fluid mixed with Jane's saliva. She made to speak, but found herself falling backwards, towards the killer sea. She fell straight into the strong, brown arms of Antonio. And something else. A force in the deep cleft of her cheeks. Her mouth fell open, her eyes closed. When she opened them again, the world had altered. Slightly. Fatally. Both the woman before her and the man behind her had become totally naked. There was a mirror between herself and the woman. She too, was nude. She was her mother's mother. Her daughter reached forward and grabbed her nipples. Working them, pulling, circling, pinching, suckling. The male form prodded at her rear, eliciting a torrent of sex-grease, urine and shit to shoot out, one after the other, onto his waiting verge. She felt his bag push, ready to explode, against her pussy as the thick, cruel veins which ran along the shaft pulsed maddeningly at the portal of her arsehole. With a single, inhuman swoop, he was in. She screamed as she felt her rear-hole split open. She let go of the large shit which had been sitting higher up in her gut. It slid down all of their four legs, coating them in excrement. The man inhaled, and roared. Her daughter-mother worked on her nipples till they bled milk. Her breasts ballooned to a size she had never before attained, and the younger, older woman bit into the tender flesh, milking the blood from the hard berries of the bouncing white cow. With her pincer nails, Lucy tugged on Jane's nipples and then arched her body forcing the younger woman to mimic the curve. They formed a diabolic line: the man's long legs, bent slightly at the knees; the invisible cock ramrodding into her; her own buttocks, firming and pushing in unison with the muscular thighs behind hem; her arched, gleaming torso, tautened beyond death's rigour; her fruit dugs, brought so skilfully to ripening point; and finally, the elegant, animal form of Lucy-Jane, as it leaned forwards, pulling on the flesh of the bitch-beast before her. Forwards and down, forwards and down. Tearing and being torn. Moving her own thighs apart, she thrust the bitch's mouth down onto her pussy, which by now was dripping with sticky sex-fluid. At first, the female simply remained there, motionless, impassive. Like a dead person. But Antonio's thrusts were growing more powerful with each fuck and her lips were being forced against Lucy's lips, petal upon petal, daughter upon mother. As she fought for breath amidst the humid jungle of Lucy's swollen cunt, her tongue involuntarily prodded at the bulging sex-organ of her mother. Lucy moaned with a pleasure she'd never even been able to dream of, before this molten afternoon in the noisy cove. Jane's body emanated choked gurgles and wet slopping sounds, from both front and behind, as her tongue welled into Lucy's vagina. She was recognising the smell, the taste, the touch, the sound of whence she had issued. She was the living circle of thrust-return-thrust. Jane had become a great red, bursting cunt-cock, a pulsating piece of flesh, the very animal glory of incest without guilt. They were the curve of Diabolos. The line took the form of an S-shape. The shape of infinity. The soul of the snake. The snake of the soul. The hot jissom exploded into her gut. Burning waves surged from arsehole to pussy to breast-tips. Seven times, she orgasmed. Seven joyous, suicidal climaxes. She arched till every joint in her fucked young body cracked and dislocated, till she, too became a twisting, swirling form upon the sand's glass face. Till she, too became the snake.

Later that same day, the younger woman took the first plane she could, out of Portugal. She knew that if she stayed, even overnight, she would never have been able to leave.

δδδδδδδδδδδδ

It was winter again when Lucy asked Rachel where the white man lived.

Melanie Desmoulins

"I have no idea," Rachel replied with a kind of off-handedness that reminded Lucy suddenly of Kent. Strange, she hadn't thought of England in a long while. Three years it must have been, since her first meeting with the dog-man and in that time, it were as though she had never had any other life than the one which she now enjoyed. Rachel went on,

"He just meets me when we arrange it. I don't know where he comes from, nor where he goes to."

She paused, as if pondering.

"...Wait a minute... he mentioned something about some village, once... 'Zambujal', I think it was. Up in the Alemtejo. Back-of-beyond."

Again, Lucy was reminded of England. She shivered. Ghosts take a long time to die, she thought. Rachel seemed not to have noticed.

"Maybe he's from there. Maybe not. I don't recall. Anyway, if it's for drugs, I can get them for you."

"No, it's not that."

"Then what?"

"Rachel, when did you first meet him?"

"Oh... sometime after I arrived here. Although, to tell you the truth, it was like I had known him before, somewhere."

"I know what you mean. And yet, when I try to picture him – his face, I mean – I can't. Only his hands. Those long, white hands with their rings and their bones."

Rachel seemed to lose interest. She didn't have the ability to concentrate for long on anything. Lucy figured it must be all the years of drink and drugs. Rachel was a loser.

"I never was any good with faces."

She smiled and as she did so, the hollow in her soul opened up.

It was time for a trip to Zambujal.

δδδδδδδδδδδδ

As she drove, she tried again and again to picture the face of the man whom she sought in the barren hills of Alemtejo. The air was cool. Not cold, but cool like that of a hill-fort sixty years ago. It were as if the air was waiting for the sun to break its beams upon the clear emptiness, so that Lucy felt she might be at the top of a mountain or else on the island in a lake. Winter in Alemtejo was short but brutal. Cold steel. A stab to the heart. No tourists ever got this far in and if they did, they ceased to be tourists but grew languid like lizards in the snow. This was where thought stopped and congealed in painter's oil, this was where life dried in the wind and the twinkle of sea fast became imaginary. This was where truths were laid bare and if found wanting, were blown to dust across the broad, brown plains. Rachel had known this – that was why she had drowned herself in wine and stuck herself with drugs. Antonio knew – his total immersion with sensual romance was as a veil across the truth. And what *was* the truth? Only Bartolomeo knew. His blank, white face knew. There was no good, no evil, no heaven, no hell, no tragedy, no comedy, no paradise, no afterlife, no beforelife, no guilt, no remorse, no justice. There was only death and life and death. That was the only certainty. That was the nothing within the nothing. The truth.

The gleaming white anthill village perched atop a dusty mound in the yellow air. She drove the car into second gear as the dust coursed past her. She tried not to inhale the foul dry mud. The courtyard was utterly bereft of shade. All of the houses were shuttered and no sound issued from outside the car. She turned off the engine, sending silence into the world with the flick of a key. She got out. The village was deserted. It was mid-afternoon. Siesta-time.

In a bar where darkness dripped from the sunlight and she was the only woman among invisible men, she ordered an anise and asked about Bartolomeo. She downed the drink in one gulp, and ordered another, and then another. She began to spin gently with the shadows and her body grew moist with the salt of the ocean. Out in the street she bumped into a bearded man carrying a guitar. It was an odd place to find a busker, she thought. He nodded wordlessly at her. Then the oddness faded away as he sat down and began to play. In the cold, dusty street, he cajoled the acoustic notes up into the blue air. The sounds which he drew from the dead, wooden instrument issued from deep in the soul of the old country, the land of Moors and Visigoths, of faith and wondrous miscegenation. The white monster walls arched and waxed as the notes of saddest blood fell from each string. His eyes were upon her.

She struggled to get away and yet...

He was plucking her with his finger-tips and his fingers were Antonio's. A shiver ran all around her spine, crushing her in coil upon coil, not letting go. Soon she would be paralysed. Thrusting her hand into her pocket, she pulled out a coin and flung it at the man. He did not acknowledge her as she almost ran from the sounds of flamenco blue.

The house was hidden between houses, white in the midst of white. A virginal village. The entrances were all small and narrow like the suspicious slits of a nun, and were barred by heavy wooden doors. She knocked, though there was no knocker. A long pause ensued during which Lucy noticed the lack of birdsong and butterfly wing in the midst of the day's belly. A small man-servant opened the door and beckoned her in. He did not wait for her to say,

"Lucy Thomas. Is Senor Bartolomeo in?" but she said it, nonetheless.

He did not reply. His eyes were flat and dull as though they had never seen youth. She had seen that sunless, empty look before. She followed the hollow man.

Once inside the house, she realised the reason for the apparent narrowness of the entrance. There were no windows whatsoever and some five yards into the building, the room broadened suddenly and giddyingly so that it felt as though she were entering a dark cave or a velvet pouch. Dim lights were everywhere – in wall-nooks, upon antique wooden tables, hanging from the low, brown ceiling – and they cast their fans in aged yellow across the rampant vermilion of the room. It all seemed so old. She sat down on a soft velvet settee. She realised that her legs, while not quite crossed, had become poised like the twin hands of a nun at prayer. This disturbed her but somehow she did not feel able to move. Without her noticing, the dull-eyed man had already slipped away. Lucy was left gazing at the obsolete round world which sat upon a table to her right. Beside the globe, there lay maps of long-defunct empires separated by dragons the size of mountain ranges and serpents the length of rivers. Gilt and leather-bound books were piled one upon another in a far corner bookcase while plantless jardinières were scattered like barren women around the room. The smell of the past reeked in her nostrils. The Portuguese past. Virgins and dictators, empires of black and canvas, miscegenation by the boatload, the scent of gentle decay...

"I am glad you have come. I knew you would. You, alone were capable of it."

Lucy spun round.

A man clad in black was standing by the globe. One hand was spinning it around while the face bore a half-smile. Both hand and smile were paper-white. Lucy wanted to rise. Not to shake hands, but simply to not feel dominated by this strange albino. But she remained where she was with her convent legs and her silence. He went over to a sideboard and poured two glasses of red wine. As she took the glass from him, his cold fingers slipped over hers. The tails of reptiles. She shuddered inwardly but managed to keep her composure. She began to feel very English. She hadn't felt that in a long time. He sat down in a large armchair opposite her. His eyes were quite pink. Again, the half-smile which she thought now was more like a sneer. Perhaps it was the way his face was made.

"How did you know I would come?"

"How did *you* know you would come?"

She paused. He sounded different from before. His accent was elegant, like a trill or an adagio as though he belonged to another century, a different world. She wondered which was the real one, and which the act.

"Who are you – to Rachel and Antonio? Why are you always hanging around the edges?"

He drank. She took a sip. The wine was strong. Blooded. She wondered how such a pale person could possibly ingest so red a substance. Perhaps he was red, inside. He gestured towards a large painting which Lucy hadn't noticed before. It hung in semi- darkness upon the far wall in the deepest recess of the room.

"For all the answers to all of the earth, one need look no further."

Suddenly she found herself on her feet. The painting was cast in dark oils and yet a yellow glow seemed to emanate from behind the canvas. She wondered how the artist had achieved that effect. The scene was a triptych, much in the manner of old medieval paintings. She found herself drawn down to the faces of the figures on her left. Every century has its own visage. It was not so much in the bone structure – such things, after all, did not change from one ape to another – but rather, in the shadows of light cast

---

Melanie Desmoulins

upon skin, in the gleam of eye, in the hunch of neck upon spine, the force in the blood of the veins. The men and women in this section of the triptych all seemed to be setting off on a journey of some sort. Upon their faces, there skimmed a mixture of despair and hope. Among them were the whore and the man who had been tied to a boulder, and behind them were the two cannibal women with white skin and between them, their victim, the olive-skinned youth. And there, at back of all, were the couple who had been humping in the doorway, back on that rainy night so long ago. The rough ground upon which they trod was inclined upwards by the very slightest of degrees. So marginal was the slope, that when Lucy closed her left eye, it appeared flat. For once you were on the hill, you did not notice that it was a hill. With her right eye, she had made a choice to mount the slope along with the beggars, priests and widows of the painting. In the background lay the tiny shapes of houses, a church, a flotilla of sailships, and in the far distance there hovered an old moon. Tarnished, tired. As we all grow at last to one another. Familiar, contemptible. Lucy turned away, writhing with disgust. The central portion of the painting resembled a sea which began in deepest black and which grew ever more blue until at the end, it was the colour of a Roman sky. But the strangest things were the creatures which swam through the boatless sea. The people of the earlier section fell from a cliff into the black water where, for a time, they disappeared into nothingness. Then, as she moved along the scene, there emerged from the darkness odd, eyeless creatures covered in scales of vermilion and gold and possessed of a single fin. And yet, the faces were recognisable as those of the multitudes who had set off from village and brothel, lake and nunnery. But they were not alone in the darkness. Following them, and goading them on were tiny demon figures who looked like a cross between satyrs and fish. In their fin-hands, they wielded tridents and on their faces were uniform half-smiles. Like the swimmers, they were pale to the point of absolution. But the demons had eyes. Pink eyes. Towards the far end of the central section, the swimmers clambered up onto a beach of blood-coloured sand. Lucy turned her eyes toward the last scene, and her body followed. It was framed in red, as if the embers of a dying fire were somehow burning behind the wall. The people had resumed their former shapes but were now entirely naked and were even whiter than before. Their pink eyes bore no expression and they were almost bald. However, the bulges on their bodies were exaggerated so that the women's breasts had grown to an obscene size, running down their bellies to rest upon their knees. Their buttocks fanned out behind them like old cartoons of Bantu tribeswomen. The men were possessed of enormous phalluses and ball bags the size of purses. All were in erection. As she looked further still, the women and men had begun to perform with one another. The women doing fellatio, the men, cunnilingus, while bodies were impaled in impossible positions and through every imaginable orifice. Males clambered onto the backs of other males, while the legs of females sinewed amongst one another like long, white jungle-stems. And then there were the beasts. Dogs, hares, horses, deer, bears, apes – all were engaging in sexual concourse with the villagers. Pools of milk mingled with the ponds of water while rice paddies swarmed amongst a forest of trees adorned with creepers. Above the scene and yet on the same level with it depthwise, there fluttered silent flocks of doves, cuckoos, parrots, pigeons, quails, bees, sparrows, ducks and other flying things which Lucy could not define. And at the very far end of the painting, there stood a naked, bull-headed being with the legs of a man and the phallus of a lion. A red sun shone from behind his horns. Lucy shuddered, and yet at the same time, she felt the quiver of arousal spark somewhere in her pelvis.

"What a strange painting..." she began but then she noticed Bartolomeo's hand on her shoulder. She wasn't sure how long it had been there. She felt the claw fingers through her cotton dress, the ooze of ages as it slipped through the veil of today.

"It is, as you make it," he replied, quietly. It was Antonio's voice, behind her. She spun round. In the visage before her were many faces: the face of the man as he glanced up from the dark doorway, the face of the whore as she sucked her hundredth client that night, the screaming, tortured jowl of the boulder-breast, the trapped face of the duped youth, frozen forever at the height of orgasm. Rachel's enticing lips, Jane's flat tones... Jane? Had she, too been here, Lucy wondered. Perhaps in a dream. She had seen no serpent ring upon her daughter's finger. But then, it was she who had bought the ticket in the first place. Peter's face was not among them.

The albino was smiling a half-smile.

"Follow me," he commanded, with his eyes.

She felt she had no choice. The very thought of choice, of decision had been taken away from her so that she could no longer conceive of what it meant. It felt good. She saw her face reflected in the painting as it faded back into darkness. She had made her choice a long time ago. Just like those villagers.

He showed her into a room upstairs. It smelled musty. There was a bed and a cabinet filled with old books. He left her without saying anything. She went over to the books. They were old and bound in soft leather. Gold lettering was inscribed upon their spines. Some were untitled. She stretched up for one of these. It was just beyond her reach. Using the ends of her fingers, she managed to tilt it slightly, so that it fell into her hand. It seemed to tremble like a bird as she took a firm hold upon its leathered back. Lucy lay on the bed and began to leaf through the pages. They smelt of young bones.

The Strange Case Of The Carthusian Sister

Once on a daye longe remov'd from any knowne to this centurie or t'one before it, there was born'd into the forest a girle who was giv'n the nom, Martha. Her father was but a woodcutter, and her mother a seamstress. One daye when she had pass'd but six years of her life, while at play in the heart o' the forest, she did chance upon a small clearing. Therein did she witness her father rutting a hog which squeal'd moste miserable with delighte which assuredly only a dumbe beast can knowe. From that daye on, the girle forfeited the power of speech, that moste God-given of virtues bestow'd unto this curs'd race know'd as Man. No soul knew t'reason for her forfeiture, and as folkes have want to do, they suppos'd her to be feeble-minded, or such like. Because of her lacke of sounde, Martha was able to tread moste lightlie'pon leaf and twig, alike and was thus permitted by fate to espie'pon every doing, bon and heinous, in the forest. And so did this virtuous being witness the bursting of bud into flow'r, the spinning of spiders' web, the coupling of woman with man – sometime like with like, sometime with opposite – and the joining of both with beasts of fielde and forest. And when the time came for her to seek a husband, it was cleare to all and sundrie that no man would ever touch her. Such was their fear of the mute. And so her lot would have been a tragic one

---

indeede, had not a kindly parish priest look'd fondlie'pon her golden head and gently suggested that she enter into wedlock wi' one who'd ne'er taunt her cunny, none other than Our Dear Lord Jesus, himself. And what better, for one made mute by this life than to be taken up by the Silent Order Of Carthusian Sisters. And so, with much weeping and sobbing (though not from her owne lip, nor from her owne throate), Martha was turn'd, by degrees into a Bride Of Christ. She went unto this fate of hers moste meekly and her countenance was possess'd of a smile so beautific that the very bulls did pause in their devilish pursuits to gape at her spectacle. She did indeede glean no inconsiderable joy from knowing that henceforth would she be dwelling at last amongst companie of a nature moste similar to her owne.

She advanced through Postulancy, Novitiate and Temporary Vows without demur and at last was granted entry to the select Convent of Ste. Isidora Of Sevilla as a Life Professed Carthusian Sister. One daye, while strolling through the forest which surrounded the old convent, Sister Mary (for such was she now know'd) came upon a pair of hogs in the very act of rutting. Sister Mary stood, transfix'd by the spectacle and when the pigs had finish'd their bestial business, she carefully stripp'd herself of all her clothing and offer'd her owne behinde to the male of the couplet. Not a little astonish'd, the beaste promptly began to rut her in similar manner as he had, the one of his owne specie. For'tis well know'd that no couple among beasts resemble each other in that area of the body know'd as the cunny as doth the woman and the female of the hog. When he had done with her — which was more faster than she had suppos'd, since dumbe beasts knowe not of the pleasures of that glorious creation which is know'd by some as, 'afore playe' — the foule pigman ran off, howling with triumph, into the blacken'd forest. Possess'd of great ceremony, Sister Mary donned her ecclesiastical robes amidst the deepest of silences and made her way back to the Convent where she join'd Convectual Mass.

From that day on, nothing within the Convent was the same. One by one, Sister Mary seduc'd and laid low the brides of Christ and when she had despoil'd the flower of womanhood, she turn'd to the neighbouring monks and priests who, it muste needes herein be said, were not slothe in conjoining wi' the golden nun. The children she bore, 'tis said, did take the forms of halfhogs and ran off,

Melanie Desmoulins

dripping and squealinge into the forest where they set up a colonie of bandits moste foule. On her verie deathbed, many years later, 'tis said Sister Mary did entice even her Father Confessor to bestride her and neigh in t'manner of a stallion or donkey. She perish'd silently as she had liv'd, at the very height of this life and if Hell is where she is destin'd to rest, then assuredly it muste needs be a silent hell, for in such a noiseless ear was her damnation conceiv'd. Once in that glorious abode which is know'd as 'Hell', the Martha, Sister Mary didst meet and have concourse wi' the spirite know'd as 'The Wyve Of Bathe' who was acqauint'd, 'tis sure, wi' him know'd as 'Geoff Of The Chaussiers' who didst tarrie in that same place while drown'd in a bott o' the wyn.

Lucy flicked the pages over and then laid the book down on the broad bed, allowing the book to dictate where it next opened. A strange, sweet odour emanated from the old paper, the same smell which had puzzled her ever since she had entered the house. A quiver of delicious anticipation slithered through her body. It was the stink of old coition, the screaming and squirting of ancient lust. Every pore stiffened, every finger stretched out so that the joints cracked. The room wanted to slide into her. The snake-room. The total body fuck. But not yet. It was too soon. With an effort, she forced herself to look at the book once more.

I prefere a yonge man for coition, and him onlie;
And he is fulle of courage – he is my seule ambition,
His member is strong to defleur the virginie,
And richlie proportion'd in all its dimensions;
It has a tete like to a brazier.
Enorme, and none like it in creation;
Strong it is and hard, with the tete round'd off.
It is always ready for action and does not die downe;
It never dorme, owing to the violence of its love.
It sighs to enter my vulva, and sheds tears on my bellie;
It asks not for help, not being in want of any;
It has no neede of an ally, and stands seul the greatest fatigues,
And nobodie can be sure of what will result from its efforts.
Full of vigour and life, it bores into my vagina,

And it works about there in action constant and splendid.
First from the van to the rear, and then from the droite to
the gauche;
 Now it is cramm'd hard in by vigorous pressure,
 Now it rubs its tete on the orifice of mie vagina.
 And he strokes my back, my stomach, mie sides,
 Kisses my cheeks, and anon begins to suck at my lips.
 He embraces me close, and makes me roll on the bed,
 And between his arms I am like a corpse without life.
 Every part of my body receives in turn his love-bites,
 And he covers me with kisses of fire;
 When he sees me in heat he quickly comes to me,
 Then he opens mie thighs and kisses mie bellie,
 And puts his toole in mie main to make it knocke at mie
porte.
 Soon he is in the cave, and I feel plaisir approaching.
 He shaketh mie and trills me, and hotlie we both are
working,
 And he sayeth, 'Receiveth mie seed!' and I answer, 'Oh
giveth it, beloved one!*
 It shall be welcome to me, you light of mie eyes!
 Oh you man of all men, who fillest me with pleasure.
 Oh, you soul of mie soul, go on with frais vigour,
 For you muste not yet withdraw it from me; leave it there,
 And this jour will then be libre of all sorrow.'
 He hath sworne to God to have me for seventy nights,
 And what he wished for he did, in the way of kisses and
embraces, during all those nights.*

Lucy wanted to be fucked by the ghost of Casanova, Don Juan and all the lovers who had gone before. She wanted to open her pussy to all the cocks of bygone ages. She wanted to feel the slime of dead men slide into her body. She would be the great whore of Babylon. Yes! The Salome, the Jezebel, the Mary Magdalene of the ages. Yes! Yes! She would be the gleaming cunt of gypsies enticing young men away from their boring families. She would give birth to changelings. Demon-children. Yes! Yes! Yes!

 Lucy wiped the sweat from the back of her neck. As she did so, the book, newly-freed, blew in the thrall of some invisible wind

  Melanie Desmoulins

to yet another section, entitled:

The Storie Of The Mule
 There was once a woman living in the times of the Maures who tooke to wandering on all fours in the wilds of Alem-Tejo. She was found there one nighte by two old trolles who proceeded to impale her from bothe ends with their foot-long phalluses. When all was goode and finish'd, they left her barren like the lande. For many year, she sought after the beastes of the field know'd t'all and sundrie as 'mules'. For these were barren liken to herselfe and so the only offspring of such infernal unions would not be in this worlde, but in the nexte.

A gentle breeze lifted the tress of Lucy's skirt. She was naked beneath. The window was open, just a crack and she went over and swung it wide and let her eyes close. The cool wind of the plains dried her sweat and made her hairs stand on end. Behind the redness of her lids, the ancient liquids flowed and merged and her head began to spin. Amidst the warm cold of the river wind were there words fashioned.

Woman is like a fruit, which will not yield its sweetness until thou rub it between thine hands. Look at the basil plante; if thou do not rub it warm with thine fingers it will not emit any scent. Dost thou not know that the amber, unless it is handl'd and warm'd, keepeth hidden within its pores th'aroma contain'd within it. 'Tis the same wi' woman. If thou dost not animate her with thy toying, intermix'd wi' kissing, nibbling and touching, thou wilt not obtain from her what thou art wishing; thou wilt feel no enjoyment when thou shareth her couche, and thou wilt waken in her coeur neither inclination nor affection, nor love for thee; all her qualities will remain hidden.

The Storie Of The Castrati
 There was once a choir of castrati. They were the beste in the worlde, this side of Hell. They achieved this magnificente feat onlie through the moste heinous of acts. Everie nighte, loud screams of terror and excruciating pain would issue from the castle in which they did have abode. Every nighte, they would grow full manlie

---

pudenda, only to have the selfsame torn off with neither mercy nor humanitie by the teeth of long-dead lions, the selfsame beastes who, in times more past e'en than past, had been blooded wi' heart's blood and groin eggs of the Chretiens of Old Rome. Their screams caus'd their throats to break backward so rend'ring unto their voices that which is know'd to be possess'd onlie by the castrati.

She picked another book off the shelf. It fell open at a page which detailed the various possible positions for sexual intercourse.

Manner The First
        Make the man lie upon his back, wi' his thighs low'r'd, then, getting him between thy legs, introduce his member into thee. Pressing thy toes to the ground, thou can rummage him in a convenient, measured way. This is a goode position for a woman wi' a longe fannie.

Manner The Second
        If the man's member is a shorte one, lie thyself upon thy back, lifte thy legs in th' air, so that thy droite leg be near thy droite ear, and the gauche one near thy gauche ear, and in this posture, with thy buttocks lifted up, thy vulva will project forwarde. Then pull in his member.

Manner The Third
        Let the man stretch himself upon the ground, and place him between thy thighs; then putting one of his legs upon thine owne shoulder, and the other under thine owne arme, near the armpit, get him into thee.

Manner The Fourth
        Lie thyself downe, and put thy legs on his shoulders; in this position his member will just face thy vulva, which must not touch the ground. And then introduce his member.

Manner The Fifth
        Lie down on thy side, then lie him down by thee on his side, and getting him between thy thighs, pull his member into thy vagina.

Manner The Sixth

Get down on thy knees and elbows, as if kneeling in prayer. In this position the vulva is projected rearwards; he muste then attack thee from that side, and put his member into thee.

Manner The Seventh

Lie on thy side, and squat the man between thy thighs, with one of thine owne legs on his shoulder and t'other between his thighs, whilst thou remaineth upon thy side. Then he muste needes enter thy vagina, and cause thee to move by drawing thee towards his owne chest by means of his hands, with which he dost holde thee embrac'd.

Manner The Eighth

Stretch thyself upon the ground, with thy legs cross'd; then be mounted akin to a cavalier on horseback, the man being on his knees, while thy legs are plac'd under thy thighs, and pull his member into thy vagina.

Manner The Ninth

Place thyself so that thou leaneth wi' thy van, or, if thou preferest it, thy back upon a moderate elevation, with thy feet set upon the ground. Thou thus offers thy vulva to th'introduction of his member.

Manner The Tenth

Place thyself near to a low divan, the back of which thou can take hold of wi' thy hands; then, getting him under thee, commande him to lift thy legs to the height of his navel and to let thee clasp him wi' thy legs on each side of his bodie; in this position order him to plante his verge into thee, seizing with his hands the back of the divan. When thou beginest the action thine owne movements muste respond to those of the man.

Manner The Eleventh

Lie upon thy back on the ground with a cushion under thy posterior; then getting him between thy legs, and placing the sole of thy droite foot against the sole of thy gauche foot, commande him to introduce his member.

Lucy found herself panting uncontrollably. God, how she needed a fuck. She thought of rubbing herself flitted into her fevered mind, but she wanted to postpone things, partly because she wanted to read more – it seemed to get hotter and hotter, the more she read, and partly because she knew that the longer she held back, whatever was in store for her in this strange house would be all the more mind-blowing when it did happen. She felt that she had to be pure, in order to approach the altar of sexual heaven. It was an odd paradox, but there it was. A bit like the nuns she'd just read about. She calmed her pounding chest, and read on.

The fuckers of Hindustan, having advanced further in the art of coitus, have multiplied the positions of love. Amongst those manners are the following, called:

El Asemeud, the stopperage.
Stop me with the stopperage
El modefeda, frog fashion.
Frog me like a frog
El mokefa, with the toes cramped.
Cramp me with your toes
El mokermeutt, with legs in the air.
Legs legs legs
El setouri, he-goat fashion.
Goat-Satan, fuck my cunt
El loulabi, the screw of Archimedes.
Screw my arsehole. Now!!!!
El kelouci, the summersault.
Acrobat, come and be lesbos with me
El Hachou en nekanok, the tail of the ostrich.
Tickle me with your tail
Lebeuss el djuoreb, fitting on of the sock.
Sock, wrap thy skin around my lips
Kechef el astine, reciprocal sight of the posteriors.
The curve of thy half-moons
Neza el kouss, the rainbow arch.
Break your bones with the arch
Dok el arz, pounding on the spot.
Pound me into the ground, into dust

Melanie Desmoulins

Nik el kohoul, coition from the back.
Fuck me like a dog
El keurchi, belly to belly.
Fuck me like a dolphin
El kebachi, ram-fashion.
Fuck me like a ram
Dok el outed, driving the ram home.
Fuck me, Satan
Sebek el heub, love's fusion.
Love and lust are the same
Tred ech chate, sheep-fashion.
I want a dumb beast to couple with me
Kalen el miche, interchange in coition.
Give me three cocks at once
Rekeud el air, the race of the member.
Give me three shining cocks at once
El modakheli, the fitter-in.
Fit into me, bull
El khouariki, the one who stops in the house.
Stop inside me, bull
Nik el haddadi, the smith's coition.
I want the worker's fuck
El moheundi, the seducer.
I want the aristo's fuck

She closed her eyes, pictured all of these wonderful positions to herself. The strange twisting of limbs, the twitching of loin upon loin, the grunting, sighing and screaming. The slurping sounds of sex. Pathetic and miraculous. Divine and diabolic. The tyranny of the body. The gift of God. The passion of Satan. It was all there, in the act of sex. Nothing was more important than that. Nothing. The emptying out of self with the opening up of cunt, the spilling of seed. Sex was life. It was the state of being alive. The only things without it were either mere objects, or else were dead. And she was not dead. Nearly had been. For year upon year, she had piled the earth in spadefuls over her blind head, had rejoiced in her impending oblivion. But not now. No way. She was out to savour every last minute of life. A transformation? Perhaps. Or a revealing, more like it. A total wiping of the slate. Thousands of years of foolish prudery was about to be finally cleaned away. But it had to be right. She knew it couldn't be forced. Everything that had happened to her since she'd come to this country, had happened because it was right. She had never thought about it beforehand. It had simply occurred. She opened her eyes, and read on.

The Tale Of The Milkmaids

Twelve milkmaids, virgins all, decided one pitch night to accoste a yonge tynker on his waye home. This was because they took a liken to the eyes of the man. They fell upon him as he made his waye through the dark forest and layinge him bare as a babe, they sat upon his legs and themselves remaining motionless, they milk'd him dry. So barren did they leave him, that the lands all aboute grew harde and bitter and yielded neither fruit nor crop. The maids – no longer maids – grew fat as their cattle and so did bring upon themsleves the wroth of the populace who had begun in slow fashion, to starve. One nighte, the villagers enter'd unto the barn in whose bosom the milkmaids were sleepinge. Taking up ploughshare and sythe – the tools of their trade – they slaughter'd every one. The goode townsfolke were moste surpris'd to laie sighte'pon the vision which that did flow from their necks was not blood, but rather, milke.

The next volume she gazed at reeked of smegma and semen. Lucy inhaled. There was nothing she loved more than that scent. Primal, basic, disgusting and yet unbearably attractive. She flipped through the pages, each one smelling stronger than the one before. It were as though the book itself were attaining climax. *An orgasmic book,* Lucy thought, amusedly. Within the tome, were listed hordes of devices which might aid the acts of the flesh.

The double-headed halter
She closed her eyes and inhaled
Lucy groaned with pleasure as the thongs around her neck and pelvis forced her to crouch, dog-fashion as her master, the albino drove her on with a wrist clad in black studded leather. Running on all fours was the surest way to be free in bondage.
The microchip phallus
She closed her eyes and inhaled

Throbbing involuntarily, this appendage became the ruler of whichever cock it crowned. It made her pussy-lips bulge and swell with insatiable desire, never quite fulfilling yet always promising more, more, more!!!

The worm phallus
Inhale
Elongating with each withdrawal, this male accoutrement contracted like a fist when shoved in. Ideal for anal intercourse.

The art of anusthetics
Sniff
Anally midway between anaesthetic and aesthetic: the sudden nausea grip above her rectum; the delirious, explosive release of excreta was like anal vomiting. She was inside her own shithole. She had become the great, coiling female uroboros.

The cunt-teaser
She no longer needed to inhale
Miniature electric shocks through a dildo to the cunt muscles and also the sphincter strengthened her rings to such an extent that she knew she would be capable of sucking a man to the come-point or, if he did not please her, of ripping a male's penis off with one contraction.

The jellyfish vaginal shirt
Spineless orgasms, flagellating limbs
Spined plastic female sheath, rendering pleasure both ways before the poison released in its stings caused cardiac arrest. The ultimate orgasm.

The three modes of castration
She had been here, before. The ring of men, hanging on meat-hooks. Erect and spunked to beyond any natural climax. Beyond the orgasm of the gods. Lucy took a sharp knife – a butcher's blade, long as a lion's cock – and went up to the nearest beast. Cradling his bag in her left palm, she drew the cold, metal edge over the rough skin. The balls tautened in expectation, and the prick stiffened again. Men are such worms, she thought, and she took the silver angel of death and slit the scrotum, end-to-end. The body convulsed in agony, but no sound issued from the deeply-gagged mouth. A stream of boiling urine spat down into her mouth, now gaping in the ecstasy of the sadist. Eagerly, she gulped down the bitter piss, and began tongue-tickling the balls. Taking the small, marbled Chinese

eggs into the evil cavern of her whore's gob, she sucked them off their stalks. She chewed the jellied spheres. She tasted the maleness of their structure, their cold spermatozoa, not-yet-formed, wriggling deep in her warm throat. She had partaken of the joy and salvation of man, and now she would be greater than both man and woman. She would kiss the arse of God.

The second male, also gagged and blind-folded, had his sack torn off between incisors. The rollers within lasted less than the time it takes to spunk.

The third became the victim of her nails. The beast claws of her hands tore the limpid ball-bag from its moorings with a single movement (so adroit had she become in the art of torture).

Opening her eyes at last, she found herself to be drenched in semen. The book was sticky as hell. She ladled up great gouts of the jissom and savoured the sour opalescent fluid as it slithered down her long throat. Her skin wet and her cunt wetter still, she stood on a chair and reached up to the topmost shelf of the bookcase. A book whose binding had no writing on had caught her eye and she wanted to see what it was. Lying girl-like (she chuckled at the simile) on her bed, she opened the slim volume. Its pages were not quite yellowed but bore that pallor which is indicative of paper which has been closed in an airless cupboard or shelf for most of its life. The print was in standard black. Lucy wondered why it was, books were always in black. Why not green, or blue, or purple? She chuckled again. It was just the way she was thinking. It was her new self. Her oldest self. The self before Lucy.

My mother ran a rooming-house on the South Coast. Well, actually it was more like a bordello. A brothel. I must be honest about these things now. I have lied all my life, and now I must be honest. It will be my only virtue. It is the only virtue worth its salt. My mother was a whore. But she was not just an ordinary lamp-post lady. She was what they used to call, 'a Madam'. I don't know how she had got into that line of business – she never told me – but I suspect that once the boarding-house had been, just that. Before the War, I mean. Then the War came and the place filled up with soldiers and sailors, airmen and the like, all on leave from active duty. And we all know what happened during the War. You don't see much of that on Victory Parades. Women from the W.A.C.C.I. – 'Wacci Women'

Melanie Desmoulins

– used to arrive late at night and go out with the service-men. And then they used to come back with them. This happened all the time, all over the country. It has always happened – it's just that in time of war, things get more frantic, senses become sharpened, desires grow more desperate. Because it might be your last. Not that I've ever been in a war. This was long before my time. But I know what it's like. I've seen the empty eyes of the dead, full of longing for the things which they have missed, hollowed out by the youth which they threw away. Wasted. Well, anyway my mother turned a blind eye – no, I must be honest – she aided and abetted these liaisons, and I believe she may have been involved in some way with an airman, herself. My father had left us when I was only three years old. You know what widows are supposed to be like. Put it this way – I had a lot of uncles. After the War ended, the fighters went away, taking their money with them. But my mother, ever the business-woman, kept the place running. There's always plenty of custom to be had in a seaside resort. It's the changeable nature of the place, you see. The tide goes out, the tide comes in and with it arrive a new batch of the bored, the prurient and the plain lonely. There's no-one to judge your actions but the sea, and its not saying anything. The police kept their distance. They used it, too. I've heard that in some countries, there are up-front, legal bordellos. It wasn't quite like that. But it wasn't far off. In its heyday, quite a few big cars used to pull up in front of the four-storey building. My mother was an attractive woman of the brunette type and she would sometimes entertain clients herself. But this would only happen very occasionally. With rich clients, or perhaps very long-standing ones. It was like a contract. People always think that brothels are places of misery, exploitation and the like. You'll hear bleeding-hearts go on and on about them. As if they'd ever been in one. Put them in one, and they'd run a mile. They're like any other institution. They are, what you make of them. It's a contract, like anything else. All these people who 'fall in love' and have sex, or get married or whatever. They're all engaging in one contract, or another. They might not see it like that – in fact, they probably won't see it like that, but that's what they are doing. Whether it's a contract of lust, or of money or status. They become attracted for many reasons. But people tend to forget about the reasons. That's where the business takes place. The trade-off. You only sell your soul if at some level you have something

to gain. For example, a poor girl will often try and hook a richer man. She may not even realise she's doing it for that reason, I mean she may not be an obvious gold-digger. But it's there, nonetheless. And it works in reverse, too. Or a black man will try to stick with a white woman because that way, he'll get more respect from people. Even if the white woman treats him like shit, he'll follow her around like a faithful dog. Just because of her skin. I've seen it happen.

At first, I was not involved in the sex side of things myself, but because I lived there I had many friendships with the girls, some of whom were not much older than me. You learn a lot about human nature in the raw, as it were. Yes, and there was violence. But because it was a building and because my mother owned the building, if that happened the man never got back in. Ever. I've heard them howling at the moon, begging to be allowed back. They hate being shut out of the fold you know, but there was no way. In a funny sort of way, my mother was a kind of early feminist, I suppose. Though I'm sure they wouldn't agree with that. But then, who are they to know? They deny human emotion instead of recognising its existence. We are all from the jungle and in the jungle, anything goes. All the things we call 'sins', they're all just what we used to do – and still do – in the old forests. The demons we see are mirrors of ourselves. They are ourselves, denied. The are given life by our madness. The madness of morality. But I'm digressing. To get back to the whorehouse. I really loved it there, but when I was sixteen, I ran away. This was not because I was being forced to become a prostitute. Far from it. If I hadn't wanted to become one, I wouldn't have become one. There was no problem with that. But I did want to become one. Become is the wrong word. I grew up with sex. It was nothing to me. It was everything to me. My mother came from a long line of hookers, going back, they say, to Regency Days. Oh, I'd had my share of carnal pleasures. By the tender age of one-and-six, I'd been with as many men – and women – as anyone else will have had hot dinners. I knew everything there was to know about sex. My mother was a good teacher. A very good instructress. I remember the first time I had it, the very first time I was penetrated – my mother had asked one of her regular clients to do the job, in return for having her after he'd had me – she insisted on watching us and instructing me in the art of love. I soon became the attraction of the brothel. The Star Attraction. The hole everyone wanted –

needed – to possess. *They would be queuing at the door, only five minutes away from their boring wives and their boring children, and they be lining up to have a go at yours truly. I was the princess of the hookers, the reginissima of the whores. My steaming cunt attracted men from all over the country, from dukes to plumbers. I'm serious. I would take pride in doing everything they wanted. If they wanted to eat shit, they ate my shit. The dukes included. If they wanted me to piss on them, I'd piss on them. If they needed to have me fuck them from behind using an artificial penis, I'd do that, too. I was their dog, their pig, their elephant, their fairy godmother. But most of all, I was their snake. I loved that. It were as if I should have been a serpent, if I had not been imprisoned in this idiot body of a woman. I would slither, totally naked of course, across the room and up their fat bellies. And then I would slither right into them, into their arsehole with my toe, down their throat with my tongue, into their navel with my cunt-head. And then, I would let them slide into me. Their throbbing pricks, around my lips, their shithole into my sucking mouth, and finally, when they were almost dead from desire (I would make the dukes plead and beg like rats upon the floor; I would make them piss in their pants, I would demand they lick the soles of my feet), I would let them enter the portal which we women hold above men. Don't believe anyone who says they fake it. They may, but that doesn't mean they don't enjoy the power, both of deception and of having someone absolutely need you to the point of betraying everything they lived for. So it comes to the same thing. I loved every minute of it. Every fucking second. That's what human beings are made for, after all. Everything in us – our mind, our body, our soul – is made only for that one act, that one moment of utter abandon. We should worship that, and not some idiot god who only speaks to men with long beards and limp pricks. Yes! I worship the beast and I am proud of it.*

But I digress. OK, so I ran away. I ran away for a simple reason. I wanted to live with a rich man. And there was no shortage of those about. I wanted to feel the power of jewels down my young back, I wanted to be a possession like a ruby or a sapphire. Because I saw that people only give respect to their possessions. To their money. He was a lot older than me. Perhaps I was looking for a father-figure, I don't know. I lived in a flat which William put me up in, for seven years. During that time, I did it all. He used to bring

---

home women and boys and we used to have orgies and get totally fucked out of our minds on booze, drugs and... well, and fucking, and for a while it was great fun. Yes, it really was. Until I grew bored with it all. It's okay being a possession, so long as you're happy with the contract. Once you begin to need more, then it's time to get out. By more, I don't mean a 'meaningful relationship' like in the movies. That's bullshit. I mean other ways of giving and receiving favours. I mean, there's only so much one man can do. You know what I mean. If you're a woman, that is. And I know, if you're reading this, that you must be a woman. Anyhow, I took the jewels he'd given me and ran. I came south. I don't know why, I suppose maybe it was the thought of being in the sun, of being away from that old, stuck-up country of mine. I always wanted to make love in full view of the sun. I always wanted my cunt to get sunburn. I wanted to savour lust in a hot land. The lust of the burning earth. I wanted to cover my long legs in olive oil and make some man come within seconds of touching them. I was curious to taste the semen of the southern reaches. I needed to dance the dance of death with the bulls of Andalusia and Algarve. To run my rough tongue over the taut cocks of dying touros, to seduce the priest who had never touched even a choir-boy. I don't know. Sometimes, I think it's all been planned – this whole thing, my whole life – by whom, I haven't a clue. I remember the first time I met Bartolomeo. It was the coldest day I have ever known in this country. One might say, I felt quite at home, except I hated the cold. I always have. He was standing with his back to the sun and it made him look like a god. Then I realised I'd actually met him long before, when I was only ten years old, back in England. I hadn't known who he was, of course. He'd come up to me by the school gates – yes, I went to school even though my mother was a Madam – and he bent down and handed me a single red rose and said,

"Today you are a woman."

Come to think of it, I hadn't been at all frightened. I was used to strange men. Most of them were my uncles. But he was different. His face – so pale, his voice, so quiet. I remembered him, even though I had forgotten him. And then when he appeared in Portugal, it flipped me. I met Antonio. It was like being in a film-script – you know, the ones from the 'fifties, where pricks didn't exist (and as for cunts...) – I was 'in love' with a gorgeous man. And

Melanie Desmoulins

I married him. I swore I would be celibate. Even became a Catholic. Imagine that. Me, who had never so much as prayed to a stone, suddenly I was going to confession and chewing those awful bits of plastic or whatever they're made from nowadays. "Father, I have sinned. I have allowed the pig to engage in copulation with me. Father, please help me." It didn't last long. It was a game, anyhow. Antonio was part of Bartolomeo's great game. He wanted to find the perfect being. The most lustful, that is. Either he would get it, or else he would blow your mind with drink and drugs, or else you would just have to keep on acting – like poor Antonio. The romantic act. Bullshit. If you have got this far, then you'll have got further than me. God! I keep moving away from what I want to tell you. I ran away from one rich man into the arms of another. It happened about four of five years after I'd come here. Don't think I was celibate all that time. I had my needs, just like anybody else. But it was all just casual. Animal. This time, he was younger than me. We met through Bartolomeo. He said we would find levels of joy together which we would never have attained, separately. By this time, I was well into the drugs and the booze which I had never really been out of, since my time with William. Antonio wasn't into it so deeply but he indulged me, nonetheless. And I fell into his madness. The insanity of romance. For a while, it was fun. Like being in a play or a book or a film. Being feted all the time. We even got married. Oh, I've said that already. Now I'm beginning to repeat myself. It's the drink. Does your brain in, after a while. I'd better get on. My mother died on her back. While servicing an old client. The best way to go, they say. Usually only reserved for men, they say. Well, they're wrong. She left me bags of money, every penny gained by hard labour. The tough grind of cock on cunnie. The hardest grind of all. I shut down the whorehouse and took the money. And overnight, I became richer than my husband. Antonio is weak. At his centre, he is nothing. He drew away from Bartolomeo and so from me. He sought company with tarts and whores because they play-act all the time. He couldn't stand the whiff of reality which I had become. You see, to me, sex is not play-acting. It is deadly serious. It is worship. My god is the orgasm, my devil is the climax. They are the same. I am like Eve. I cannot tell the difference between good and evil, because they have been different in different times, in different lands. All this is in the head. But what is in the heart? I don't know.

The Snake   141

That's my problem. I have no heart, and so I can never reached the highest level to which Bartolomeo aims to take me. Drink and drugs have brought me closer to it than the fake roses of romance but I cannot get past them. Bartolomeo has turned cold since that bitch arrived. She's his new project. I lust after her with my male spirit and I lust after Antonio with my female soul and yet I despise both of them, one because he resides in dreams of ignorance and weakness, the other because I know she will go higher than I could ever go. Why? I don't know. I don't care. Yes I do. I tried destruction and I tried lust and still I am incapable of reaching that which I know is there for some. What the Hell! This is the last time I will come here, to this dust-ridden village. Let Bartolomeo pick his favourites and screw them to Purgatory. I will become an old whore with puckered nipples and floppy cunt, but there will always be those who hanker after such things. I will provide it for them, and I will take what I need from them. Because I worship sex. It is the only real proof that there is more to this shitty existence than pissing and farting. The joy that is in sex is like no other. No other. If I have to be fucked by donkeys and stray dogs in the height of summer's madness, I don't care. I am leaving.

Lucy lay back. Her arm was aching, she'd had it in the same position for so long. She eased it out, letting the pain slip from her elbow, down. So Rachel *had* been here. Somehow, she was not surprised. Of course, Rachel had lied to her. Lies were a part of the whole thing. She had to strip away the lies, one by one, and in doing so, she would become able to recognise that which was the truth. Another paradox. One among many. She wondered who else had been here. Perhaps everyone, in one way or another. Perhaps this was where Eve and Adam ran, after Eden. Perhaps this was Eden. Or maybe it was the inside of the Tree. The great big phallus of a tree which Eve had sucked on. The suck of the snake...

She fell asleep to the sight of two insects joining together on the windowsill.

δδδδδδδδδδδδ

"She was here, wasn't she?"

Bartolomeo arched his pale brows.

"Yes. Many have been here but not all see it right through."

"What happens to them – the ones who don't see it right through?"

He turned away.

"So many questions. Life just hits you, out of the blue. You never ask of life, 'What will happen next?'"

"Was Antonio here, too?"

Bartolomeo did not answer but contrived to potter around the shelves. It was a ludicrous thing to be doing, Lucy thought, in the middle of all this. And here he was, this mystical, sexual albino – dusting the furniture.

"This place collects a lot of dust. It blows in from the plains. Sometimes, it never stops. Some say it is a vision of Hell."

He had on a snake ring, identical to the one which Antonio, Rachel and Antonio's grandmother had all been wearing.

Lucy shuddered and drew her arms around her body. She remembered a time when she used to feel she was too fat for another man.

"Is it always women who come here, who are drawn here?"

He continued wiping the furniture. His back was towards her.

"What do you mean by 'women'?"

"Women – you know, for God's sake – females, ladies, *mulkera*..."

Bartolomeo nodded, slowly.

"That which you call 'woman' and that which you term 'man' – who decided this? Who says, 'this is man and this, woman'?"

Lucy smiled.

"It's obvious, isn't it?"

"No, you see, you believe in a myth. One among many. There is nothing 'obvious' in nature or in supernature."

"Look – men have pricks. Women don't."

"Is that all?"

"It's a start."

"Why not say: 'Women have breasts. Men don't.' Or: 'Women have a cunt. Men don't.'? You see, you have to turn everything upside-down to get at the core of things. To feel the essence. To suck of the fruit."

She was startled at this. Just what she'd been thinking,

before she'd fallen asleep in the room upstairs. She remembered waking to the sound of slithering...

"How do you define a house?"

"A house?"

"Yes. Define 'house'."

"I dunno... a structure made up of four walls and a roof, with windows, I suppose."

"And how do you define a 'structure'?"

Lucy thought for a moment.

"Something made-up, something built."

"Define 'made-up'."

She struggled.

"I can't."

"You see. Words fail you. 'Man' and 'woman' are merely words and they are ultimately of no use. There are many men who have no head hair. Yet they are not termed differently from those who possess it. Someone has just picked sex as a defining factor, which it is not. There is a stream running from the feminine force to the masculine force and the stream is within all beings, and all beings, whether sentient or not, are within the stream. You must free the barriers in your soul."

"You sound like a professor of something."

"I *am* a professor."

"Really?"

"I am many things, to many people."

There was a pause while Lucy felt very stupid. It was then she noticed that there were no clocks in the house. To hide her stupidity, she asked another question.

"Bartolomeo, can I ask you something? How old are you?"

"Older than you."

As he said this, Lucy saw skin draw tightly over bone and she looked away.

"Why me?"

"Stop looking for answers to everything."

I think, therefore I am. NO! NO! NO!

This made her jump. She looked up again. He hadn't opened his mouth, but the thought had flown into her brain.

"You just are. You would be, whether you thought, or not. Forget four hundred years. There are no reasons for anything."

So saying, he poured her a glass of dry sherry.

She gazed down at it.

"Drink. It's not spiked. You don't need that any more."

He led her down what seemed like hundreds of steps into the cellar. This cool, dark place was filled with wine bottles of all vintages. But she had no time to ponder on this, for he quickly took her to the rear of the cellar. Inlaid into the old brickwork, there was a metal door. Without a key, and seemingly without any effort, he tipped it open. She hesitated. His voice was soft, soothing and yet insinuating at the same time, like an ill breeze siphoning through the fissures in the walls of her soul.

"What is that which you most fear?"

In her mind, there uncoiled the image of a snake.

He nodded, slowly.

"And what is that which you love most?"

Her mind was blank.

"This is what you came here for."

His voice had fallen to the level, passionless tone of an amphibian.

It was strange, how he could alter his voice so dramatically. At times, he sounded like Antonio, at times, like Peter. She pushed the thought from her head. They entered a dark corridor. And yet, though there were no lights along the passageway, Lucy found she was able to make it out quite clearly, almost as if it were day down here behind the earth's face. Lucy found herself thinking of her previous life. Her childhood, in those counties of England which they called 'home', her nun-like courtship, her pre-ordained marriage, the birth of her daughter, her job, the killing of her husband... the emptiness which followed, the not knowing why. Why had he done it? Committed suicide. Becoming the hanged man. The rafters had been bent ever so slightly in the place where he had attached the rope. It was the first time she had said it for months, it was the first time since she had come here that she had admitted it to herself. This sunny paradise at the end of all paradises. This must be where Hell is. No, Hell was back there, with all its deaths and its not knowing why. Its blind, naked realities. All of her dreams were mirrors. Now the mirrors had become reality and she had seen herself for the first time. Allowed herself to see herself. Perhaps that's what Peter had done. Maybe he hadn't liked what he saw. Maybe that's why he'd killed himself. The emptiness which all her life, she had feared to touch. It was here in this cellar, in this house of the albino. The man without a face. She saw Antonio strutting with his gazelle legs, his member ripened like a fruit in the sun. She felt the light touch of his end-of-day beard upon her cheek, the honey taste of his lips. The musk of his sex. She felt Rachel's breasts, firm with the laxity of slow dissolution against her own nipples, she ran the tip of her tongue along the roughened palate, she felt the falling apart of a life. All of the past had been merely a preparation for this. This is what she had come here for. For something which, in her previous life she would have considered obscene. Beyond mention. Beyond thought. And now, it was her. The existence which she had led – or which had led her – seemed blind like an English sky. Out here, in here, the colours were all of the base. Of the blood, the root, the seed, the ocean. There was no compromise. The dagger drew life. And she had gone further than Antonio with his romantic madness or even Rachel with her plunge into debauchery. They were trapped in their desires. They had become segments of stimulation, pieces of ecstasy, merely. That was why she had come here, to this village, to the pale man who lay beyond the pale. He had led them all three like bulls by the nose, but only Lucy had broken free and run with him. Now she would know what he knew, now she would become what he was. The blank sheaf. The dagger would draw upon her breast the patterns of life. In the emptiness which lies beyond climax, in the vast, aching hollow of humanity, in the never-ending belly of the snake, there would she find...

Passing through the door, they entered a chamber filled with nothing but darkness. Lucy thought her eyes had already become accustomed to the lack of light in the long corridor but here, the murk was of a different order. As her eyes grew into those of a cat, the walls of the room emerged slowly from the emptiness. The chamber was circular. There were two doors, set at opposite ends. One was the entrance through which they had already come, while the other remained closed and dark and was possessed of a large brass knocker. Lucy moved closer to the wall on her right. She saw that the bare stone was covered with images in paint. It was almost like a fresco, but seemed somehow different. The background to the paintings was a uniform black, as if the figures had been drawn on velvet. A few buildings were scattered about but mainly, the scenes took place in the depths of the countryside. Some animals wandered around – bulls, goats and dogs of various sizes – and above, in what Lucy supposed to be the sky, though it was black as the earth, there flew a great white eagle with claws sharper than any she had ever seen or imagined. The animals were all in primary colours, so that some of the bulls were red, others white and still others, black. These last could be spotted by looking at their eyes. She found herself drawn to the human figures. These too, were in base shades but they all had eyes, large and white as if rolled up in the ecstasy of death. All were naked and were possessed of exaggerated genitalia. Lucy remembered the strange oil painting upstairs. The figures seemed to be of the same people but down here, they had been entirely stripped of personality. They were merely flickers on the film of Time's darkness. There, one minute. Gone the next. As she followed them around in the room's circle, they moved with her. It were as if they were being pulled around by the gleam of her eyes. It were as if she was in control of them. She felt the trembling juice of power flow through her body. Then she noticed that she was utterly naked. She wondered where she had left her clothes. But it had ceased to matter. The pale man was also nude and he stood by the door through which they had entered. His penis was long as a dog's tail and lay limp between his thin legs. His body was even whiter than his face. His eyes were pink. Flat. The door behind him was closed. She glanced back at the wall. Then she realised that he looked just like the figures in the painting. She wanted to follow it to its end. Needed to. The room was round, the painting was round. The painting wound around the room. The room was within the painting. In this place, there was no evil and no good. It was all just nature, and that which lay beyond nature. Even the martyrs in the very throes of their martyrdom had screamed with the ecstasy of the earth from which they were trying to escape. That was what Peter had done, by killing himself. Tried to get away from the animal, the bestial. But it was only through the beast of the body that the beyond could be reached. In his life of despair, Peter could never have learned that. So he died, not like a martyr but like a rat. Poisoned by a powder. A coward's death. For a long time, she had wished he had hanged himself, that the beams had cracked with the weight of his courage, that the mark be drawn in sorrow across the dead wood. Pictured it, even. Lied to herself. She saw herself, having sex with a corpse. How could she ever have loved him? Now she pitied him, as one might pity the ignorant, as the eagle once had pitied the scribe or the bull, the priest. The white figures were simply marching around a dark landscape, They were lost forever in its blind embrace. There was no above and no below. All were stuck in the same place. The fools who erected gods from stone and stone from gods. The blind who drew up codes and songs and cast their likenesses in gold so that they might see their way in the darkness that was beyond seeing. Lucy laughed out loud. The sound was harsh, the rasp of a serpent, the scrape of fish-cold scales upon black stone. She felt a shove from behind. She fell forwards. The dust tasted musty like the semen of old conquerors. Her knees scuffed on the ground. She felt his hands press down on her shoulders. His long, bony fingers tangled in the lips between her legs. His hands were all over her, moulding her, changing her, stripping her of herself. She felt her tired epidermis peel off, layer by layer until she was naked as Creation. She bathed in a bath of buffalo-milk and then had oil of hogweed scoured into her skin. She felt herself rise up in the darkness so that the circle of paint was below her, spinning. The expressionless expressions of the bone-stripped figures became the light of her eyes. A throbbing pulsed through her body, beginning and ending in the small hooded triangle beneath her bone. She felt her lips part like those of a cat. Welcoming him.

> *Lying on her back she is a dish;*
> *Turn her over, and you have a dish-cover*

She felt the serpent slide into her.

> *Once, a child danced in the light of my eyes.*
> *Now, the heaviness of death is upon my brow*

She felt the serpent pierce her being, she felt her lifeblood flow away into the darkness.

> *She has sent you coriander,*
> *White as sugar*

She would be pale like the figures, like the man. He thrust the daggersnake deep into her body and then pulled out, only to dive even deeper.

The pain was endless.

Dust bit into the quick of her nails. Small, sharp stones pierced the skin of her palms. Drawing blood. She tasted the dry earth of the snake. Her body writhed, every curve twisting upon the one below. Even her fingers were bent backwards in an orgy of pain and delight. In her gut, she rolled and twirled so that a spasm of mucous spewed out from her anus. The man licked this thick, viscid stream up with his long tongue which he then proceeded to ram into her mouth. His mouth-prick was hard like that of a great cat and yet at its end, it was forked. She tasted her own gut-juice and swallowed it with relish. A great feeling of satisfaction filled her belly. The fulfilling of the circle – from gut to arse, from mouth to gut. The curving serpent was in her and around her and she was the snake's lover. She was the snake. She felt the joy of the martyrs, the ecstasy of the damned, the blade of judgement as it slit her from end to end. The man was soundless. Without breath. Though he rutted her from behind, yet she saw his face in the wall. It was the face of Peter. The face of Antonio, of Rachel, of her daughter, of men and women and dogs she had desired from afar, of bulls she had never known, of a devil, sleek and hidden...

With its yellow eyes

Dancing

> *O, Time! Of all the dwellers here below*
> *You only elevate buffoons or fools,*
> *Or him whose mother was a prostitute,*
> *Or him whose anus as an inkstand serves*

She mounted to orgasm and as she died, the last vestiges of her life burned away in the black flame which engulfed the room.

cobra

The long swathes of the snake moved across the dusty floor as it coiled and uncoiled in a strange, writhing dance. Its two-pronged tongue flicked obscenely from its mindless mouth without pity, without anger. Cold, in the midst of heat. It had lain asleep for too long. Since the day of the tree and the apple. It had slept the sleep of demons, hot, amidst the cold, for too long.

And now it was awake.

He led her into the room of the snakes. A reflex fear shot through her body as she entered, sending a spurt of urine down from between her thighs. It trickled down her white leg in a long, twisting line of yellow. She felt the gentlest of nips at her heel, and the fear was gone. He made her lie down and allow the snakes to crawl all over her. She felt the delicious tingle of dry scale upon her ice-white skin. Every touch was an electric quiver of joy. She felt as though the entire surface of her body had become as sensitive, as aroused as her clitoris. No longer did she have to trawl joy from a button. Happiness was all around her. Her legs parted, and the serpents licked at her thighs. She felt her wetness run down into their opened mouths. Then one of them slid into her. Her back arched as she felt the muscle of the snake thrust and withdraw. Thrust and withdraw. Moans issued from her mouth, without her willing them. Another beast wriggled up her anus. The urge to defaecate wrenched her pelvis. She urinated instead, and the open mouths drank thirstily. She wondered if all the people in the painting had turned, at the end, into serpents. As if in some kind of sexual unison, all the snakes in the room were now upon her, around her, inside her. One was sucking on her button, making it swell painfully. She felt she was dying. But what a death. The snake in her anus

Melanie Desmoulins

pushed up into her gut, till it felt as though it *was* her gut. The stiff red in her vagina thrust its whole length into her, sending a murderous desire through her entire being.

The desire of the snake.

She was becoming the snake, and the snake was becoming her. She writhed with its coils, it arched with her back. She realised the creature in her anus was really just the tail-end of the same serpent whose tongue licked at her mouth. Just the tail-end of her. Her scream at orgasm was that of a reptile. Cold and endless.

He kept her in dark room for months on end. Or perhaps, for years on end. At first, she could not see or hear anything but as time went on (though in which direction, she could not tell for in the room of the snakes, a tail and a head were much the same thing), she began to make out vague shadows, distant snatchings. He would not appear before her, but would merely thrust in a bowl of raw meat and dank water through a narrow slit in the door. She never saw his hand. She lived as an animal. She would piss and shit without thinking and then wander through the trails of her excreta without knowing. She gobbled up the meat, tearing it with her sharpened teeth, and using her tongue, she slurped at the water, lolling it into her mouth and down her dry throat. At first, she would vomit, but then as she began to nibble at her own manure, she became used to ingesting filth of all kinds. The word, like all words, ceased to have meaning. And without meaning, there can be no judgement. She would move around only by crawling on her belly. She found that she could crawl up the walls like this and hang from the ceiling. This gave her body a thrill which lasted far, far longer than any orgasm. Her skin hardened with the constant rubbing against the rough stone floor and the mixture of straw, dust and shit which had become part of her. Her body was no longer lily-white. She was able to see in the dark and could hear all the creatures creeping in the earth below her.

One night (though perhaps it was day, since there was no difference), he came to her in a dream (though perhaps it was reality, since there was no difference). His body was that of God but his prick was a rearing serpent. In an instant, he was in her. Again, she had the feeling of writhing, both within herself and upon her skin and again, she came to a climax which only the bestial can attain.

When she awoke, she was outside
She lifted her head
It was a courtyard. She could not move. Her wrists and ankles were bound by blackened, dirty rope to thick, wooden posts. She was no longer a snake and her skin was lily-white once more. The sun burned upon her back. She heard footsteps from behind. She could not turn to see. She did not need to. She knew it was him. She wanted his long, inhuman cock inside her again. His slithering, forked tongue. His hypnotic yellow eyes. She writhed with desire. Her pink nipples bulged taut against the rough earth. Her soft belly ached with need. He cunt felt empty. Behind her
A sound
A searing
A pain
again
again
He was whipping her burned back with a nine-thonged whip.

"I am the whore!" she cried, "I am the great cunt. Fuck me. Hump me. Screw me. Kill me!"

The agony spread out across her and she fainted. The last thing she saw were his eyes, weaving and ducking as if in some bizarre dance. Yellow eyes. He whipped her until she was dust beneath his feet. He whipped her until the dust at his feet began to swirl around his ankles. In her faint, she climaxed seven times.
When she awoke, she was outside
A cock was in her hand
No
It was the handle of a whip.
The lash was of nine snakes.
He was lying naked and bound before her. She began to wield the lash. With every stroke, she yelled,

"I am better than you, because I was first. I was before man. I was before god."

As she whipped him, froth began to bubble from between her teeth and she grunted and screamed with the joy of inflicting pain and death on a living being. Her bulbous cunt seemed to grow and swell till it covered her entire being with its sticky juice, its

Melanie Desmoulins

throbbing, searing, burning joy. The triumph of the cunt was nigh. Bending down, she parted his legs and clamped her jaws around his sac. One sharp bite was enough. The eggs slithered into her whore's mouth. They tasted of iron and sex. They tasted of God. She chewed as she whipped, savouring the delicious, half-formed sperm as they wriggled around in her hot mouth. She swallowed the jelly and felt it sink through her gut, setting off a series of waves which led straight to her clit. But then, she was all clit. Every single part of her was one great joyous orgasm.

By the time his dust blew in circling trails around the courtyard, she had become
The snake.

ꝸꝸꝸꝸꝸꝸꝸꝸꝸ

She awoke
Alone
Cold
Dark
She got up
Stiff
Dark
Alone
Something on her hand
Cold
Metal
Smooth
She pushed
It swung open
Blind light
She cowered behind it
Squinted
She was invaded
Again
This time by the light
Beyond it
A circular room
The shape of a
Snake

The Snake 153

The walls were covered in mirrors and the roof was a hymen of alabaster.

Sunlight poured in without mercy, without humanity from all directions and as she removed the hands from her faces, she saw herself. A hundred times over. Her body was totally white. White as paper, white as snow, pale as death. Her muscles draped loosely over her skeleton like the shroud of a life. She moved closer to the mirror-walls. In the strange, merciless glow, her eyes glinted at themselves in a faint pinkish hue.

She emerged from the darkness of light into the cold blue of the day. She felt the imprint of an arm grip her from behind. She turned around, half-expecting to see the pale man at her back once again. But she knew he was gone. Flattened into stone and oil. Forever treading the black. She walked away from the dead white of the house and as the sun poured down upon her, she felt her skin begin to bubble and seethe. The rough hand of the south had reached out in its monochrome madness and touched her soul. Her figure descended the hill and made its way out across the open fields where once had stalked albino bulls and horned sheep. Time had removed them as it had wiped the figures from the walls.

Melanie Desmoulins

THE LUSTS OF THE LIBERTINES
The Marquis De Sade

The Circle of Manias, the Circle of Excrement, the Circle of Blood; three gateways to a living Hell envisaged by the Marquis de Sade as he simmered in the bowels of the Bastille. An infernal zone where Libertines are free to pursue and execute their every caprice, no matter how depraved or inhuman.

Here, in a brand new, unexpurgated and explicit translation, are the 447 "complex, criminal and murderous lusts" of the Libertines as documented by de Sade in his accursed atrocity bible *The 120 Days Of Sodom;* a catalogue of debaucheries, cruelties and pathological perversions still unequalled in the annals of transgressive literature.

DUNGEON EVIDENCE: *Correct Sadist II*
Terence Sellers

The Mistress Angel Stern presides without mercy over a New York dungeon where her slaves, the "morally insane" of modern society, obey her every whim and undergo any degradation she wills upon them.

In the closed confines of a torture zone, these paraphiliacs and sexual malcontents use her image as an object for their masturbatory depravities, craving her cruelty in an abyss of sadomasochism and bondage.

Here are the bizarre case histories, philosophies and psychopathologies of a dominatrix; a frank testament which reveals not only the drives which lead some to become slaves, but also the complex exchange of psychic energies involved in scenes of dominance and submission.

THE VELVET UNDERGROUND
Michael Leigh

Swingers and swappers, strippers and streetwalkers, sadists, masochists, and sexual mavericks of every persuasion; all are documented in this legendary exposé of the diseased underbelly of '60s American society.

The Velvet Underground is the ground-breaking sexological study that lent its name to the seminal New York rock'n'roll group, whose songs were to mirror its themes of depravity and social malaise.

Welcome to the sexual twilight zone, where the death orgies of Altamont and Helter Skelter are just a bull-whip's kiss away.

VELVET PUBLICATIONS

SISTER MIDNIGHT *Jeremy Reed*

The Marquis de Sade is dead – but his sister is alive and well, stalking the ruins of the château of La Coste where she reconstructs the apocalyptic orgies, tortures and blasphemies of her brother's reviled last will and testament, *The 120 Days Of Sodom.*

Castle freaks, killing gardens, lesbian love trysts on human furniture; these and countless other configurations of debauched carnality conspire and collude in a sundered, dream-like zone where the clock strikes eternal midnight.

Sister Midnight is the sequel to Jeremy Reed's erotic classic *The Pleasure Château,* a continued exploration of decadent extremes and sexual delirium in the tradition of de Sade, Sacher-Masoch and Apollinaire; a tribute to undying lust and the endless scope of human perversion.

THE SNAKE *Melanie Desmoulins*

When Lucy, a sexually frustrated young widow, is mysteriously sent a plane ticket to Portugal, she takes a flight into erotic abandon which can only lead to death and damnation.

Soon seduced by both a debauched Englishwoman and her Portuguese husband, she sheds the skin of morality like a snake and begins to act out her darkest, uninhibited sexual desires. Increasingly depraved rituals of narcotics abuse, Satanism and sadomasochism – presided over by Bartolomeo, a Sade-like albino cult leader – eventually lead to the total disintegration of Lucy's ego.

At Bartolomeo's isolated villa, a shrine to pornographic art and literature, she finally enters the snake pit...

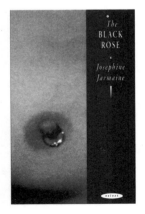

THE BLACK ROSE *Josephine Jarmaine*

Abducted to a mysterious French island, sixteen-year-old Rosamund finds herself at the mercy of the Duke and his four libidinous sons. She soon learns that her virginity must be sacrificed in order to breed the Black Rose, a rare flower whose aphrodisiac elixir will transform the world into a polysexual playground of orgiastic and orgasmic excess.

Rosamund's carnal initiation plunges her into a vortex of pain and pleasure, as she discovers that the Château Rose is a sensory realm where sadism, sapphism, sodomy, incest, bestiality, bondage and rampant fornication are a way of life.

The Black Rose is a stunning hybrid of decadence and explicit sexuality, a unique modern classic.

PHILOSOPHY IN THE BOUDOIR *The Marquis de Sade*

In the boudoir of a sequestered country house, a young virgin is ruthlessly schooled in evil. Indoctrinated by her amoral tutors in the ways of sexual perversion, fornication, murder, incest, atheism and complete self-gratification, she takes part with growing abandon in a series of violent erotic orgies which culminates with the flagellation and torture of her own mother – her final act of liberation.

Philosophy In The Boudoir is the most concise, representative text out of all the Marquis de Sade's works, containing his notorious doctrine of libertinage expounded in full, coupled with liberal doses of savage, unbridled eroticism, cruelty and violent sexuality. The renegade philosophies put forward here would later rank amongst the main cornerstones of André Breton's Surrealist manifesto.

THE SHE-DEVILS *Pierre Louÿs*

A mother and her three daughters...sharing their inexhaustible sexual favours between the same young man, each other, and anyone else who enters their web of depravity. From a chance encounter on the stairway with a voluptuous young girl, the narrator is drawn to become the plaything of four rapacious females, experiencing them all in various combinations of increasingly wild debauchery, until they one day vanish as mysteriously as they had appeared.

Described by Susan Sontag as one of the few works of the erotic imagination to deserve true literary status, *The She Devils (Trois Filles De Leur Mère)* remains Pierre Louÿs' most intense, claustrophobic work; a study of sexual obsession and mono-mania unsurpassed in its depictions of carnal excess, unbridled lust and limitless perversity.

THE PLEASURE CHATEAU *Jeremy Reed*

The story of Leanda, mistress of an opulent château, who tirelessly indulges her compulsion for sexual extremes, entertaining deviants, transsexuals and freaks in pursuit of the ultimate erotic experience. She is finally transported to a zone where sex transcends death, and existence becomes a never-ending orgy of the senses. The book also includes *Tales Of The Midget*, astonishing erotic adventures as related by a dwarf raconteur versed in decades of debauch.

Jeremy Reed, hailed as one of the greatest poets of his generation, has turned his exquisite imagination to producing this masterpiece of gothic erotica in the tradition of de Sade, Apollinaire and Sacher-Masoch, his tribute to the undying flame of human sexuality.

FLESH UNLIMITED *Guillaume Apollinaire*

The debauched aristocrat Mony Vibescu and a circle of fellow sybarites blaze a trail of uncontrollable lust, cruelty and depravity across the streets of Europe. A young man reminisces his sexual awakening at the hands of his aunt, his sister and their friends as he is irremediably corrupted in a season of carnal excess.

Flesh Unlimited is a compendium edition of *Les Onze Mille Verges* and *Les Mémoires d'Un Jeune Don Juan*, Apollinaire's two wild masterpieces of the explicit erotic imagination, works which compare with the best of the Marquis de Sade.

Presented in brand new translations by Alexis Lykiard (translator of Lautréamont's *Maldoror*), these are the original, complete and unexpurgated versions, with full introduction and notes.

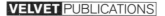

THE WHIP ANGELS *Anonymous*

Victoria's journal reveals her darkest secrets, her induction into a
bizarre yet addictive sexual underground at the hands of her immoral,
incestuous guardians. Behind the façade of everyday life seethes black
leather mayhem, voluptuous eruptions of demonic angels from
timeless torture zones, a midnight twist heralded by the bullwhip's
crack and the bittersweet swipe of the cat.

Blazing with erotic excess and incandescent cruelty, *The Whip
Angels* is a feast of dominance and submission, of corrupted
innocence and tainted love. In the tradition of *The Story Of O* and *The
Image*, this modern classic was written by an anonymous French
authoress (believed to be the wife of Georges Bataille) fully versed in the
ways of whipcord and the dark delirium of those in both physical and
spiritual bondage.

HOUSE OF PAIN *Pan Pantziarka*

When a young streetwalker is picked up by an enigmatic older
woman, she finds herself launched on an odyssey of pleasure and
pain beyond measure. Lost in a night world, thrown to the lusts of her
anonymous captors, she must submit to their increasingly bizarre
rituals of pain and degradation in order to embrace salvation.

House Of Pain is scorched earth erotica, an unprecedented glimpse
of living Hell, the torments and raptures of a young woman
abandoned to the throes of rage, violence and cruelty which feed the
sexual impulse. Churches, hospitals, courtrooms, all become mere
facets of the same unyielding edifice, a bedlam of desire and flesh in
flame beneath the cold black sun of her own unlimited yearnings.

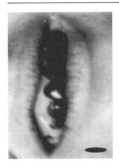

IRENE'S CUNT *Louis Aragon*

First published in France in 1928, *Le Con d'Irène ("Irene's Cunt")* is the last
lost masterpiece of Surrealist Erotica. The author of this enigmatic and
scandalous work is now known to be the great Surrealist Louis Aragon.
Like Georges Bataille's *Story Of The Eye*, written the same year, *Irene's Cunt*
is an intensely poetic account, the story of a man's torment when he
becomes fixated upon the genitalia of an imaginary woman and is reduced
to voyeuristically scoping 'her' erotic encounters.

In between describing various events in brothels and other sexual
adventures, Aragon charts an inner monologue which is often reminiscent
of Lautréamont, and of Artaud in its evocation of physical disgust as the
dark correlative to spiritual illumination. This new edition features an
exceptional and completely unexpurgated translation by Alexis Lykiard,
and includes complete annotation and an illuminating introduction.

PSYCHOPATHIA SEXUALIS *Krafft-Ebing*

Lustmurder, necrophilia, pederasty, fetishism, bestiality, transvestism and
transsexuality, rape and mutilation, sado-masochism, exhibitionism; all
these and countless other psychosexual proclivities are detailed in the 238
case histories that make up Richard von Krafft-Ebing's legendary
Psychopathia Sexualis. Long unavailable, this landmark text in the study
of sexual mania and deviation is presented in a new, modern translation
highlighting the cases chosen by Krafft-Ebing to appear in the 12th and
final edition of the book, the culmination of his life's work compiled
shortly before his death.

An essential reference book for those interested in the development of
medical and psychiatric diagnosis of sexual derangement, the
Psychopathia Sexualis will also prove a fascinating document to anyone
drawn to the darker side of human sexuality and behaviour.

VELVET PUBLICATIONS

HEAT *Candice Black (editor)*

A compendium of erotic and sex-related photography, art and literature, featuring selections from past, present and future *Velvet* publications as well as material unique to this edition.

Photography: Richard Kern, Araki, Romain Slocombe, Peter Whitehead and Simon Starkwell, plus '70s porno cinema.

Writing: the Marquis de Sade, Terence Sellers, Lydia Lunch, Jeremy Reed, Peter Sotos, Krafft-Ebing and many others.

Graphic art: the complete 50-page version of Romain Slocombe's underground S/M classic *Prisoner Of The Red Army!*.

TORTURE GARDEN *David Wood (Editor)*

From Bodyshocks to Cybersex...A Photographic Archive of the New Flesh

A unique, definitive and breath-taking 5-year photographic record of Torture Garden – described by Marquis magazine as "the world's largest and probably most famous fetish club".

This deluxe book explores and celebrates the boundaries of the body and human sexuality with an extraordinary collection of images by the scene's two leading photographers, Jeremy Cadaver and Alan Sivroni.

An extensive collection of literary quotes juxtaposed with these stunning photographs helps create an anthropological, psychological and cultural backdrop to Torture Garden's position at the frontier of the fetish/body art phenomenon. The book includes some 350 original photographs, with over 50 colour plates.

BABY DOLL *Peter Whitehead*

1972 found Rolling Stones documentarist Peter Whitehead ensconced in a chateau in southern France with a teenage heiress model and a month's supply of film and psychedelic drugs. The startling results, never before published, are contained in *Baby Doll*, a beautiful yet disturbing visual diary of a lost four weeks spent in the pursuit of both physical and spiritual erotic extremes.

An uncensored, unflinching photographic journal of sexual metamorphosis and personality disintegration, *Baby Doll* is also a unique testament to Peter Whitehead's experimental vision, a forbidden legacy of an era simultaneously marked by its innocence and its license to explore previously uncharted areas of sexuality and psychic experimentation.

CITY OF THE BROKEN DOLLS *Romain Slocombe*

Tokyo metropolis. Both in hospital rooms and on the neon streets, beautiful young Japanese girls are photographed in plastercasts and bandages, victims of unknown traumas. These are the "broken dolls" of Romain Slocombe's Tokyo, a city seething with undercurrents of violent fantasy, fetishism and bondage.

Not since J G Ballard's legendary *Crash* have the erotic possibilities of trauma – real or imagined – been so vividly exposed. *City Of The Broken Dolls* is a provocative, often startling Photographic document of a previously unseen Tokyo, and of the girls whose bodies bear mute witness to the city's futuristic, erotic interface of sex and technology.

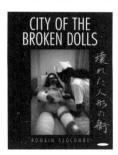

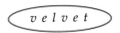

INFORMATION

You have just read a *Velvet* book
Published by:
Velvet Publications
83, Clerkenwell Road, London EC1R 5AR
Tel: 0171-430-9878 Fax: 0171-242-5527
E-mail: velvet@pussycat.demon.co.uk

Velvet publications should be available in all proper
bookstores; please ask your local retailer to order from:

UK & Europe: Turnaround Distribution, Unit 3
Olympia Trading Estate, Coburg Road, Wood Green,
London N22 6TZ
Tel: 0181-829-3000 Fax: 0181-881-5088

Italy: Apeiron Editoria & Distribuzione
Pizza Orazio Moroni 4
00060 Sant'Oresta (Roma)
Tel: 0761-579670
Fax: 0761-579737

USA: Subterranean Company, Box 160, 265 South 5th
Street, Monroe, OR 97456
Tel: 541-847-5274 Fax: 541-847-6018

USA Non-booktrade: Xclusiv, 451 50th St, Brooklyn,
NY 11220
Tel: 718-439-1271 Fax: 718-439-1272
Last Gasp, 777 Florida St, San Francisco, CA 94110
Tel: 415-824-6636 Fax: 415-824-1836
AK Distribution, PO Box 40682, San Francisco,
CA 94140-0682
Tel: 415-864-0892 Fax: 415-864-0893

Canada: Marginal, Unit 102, 277 George Street, N.
Peterborough, Ontario K9J 3G9
Tel/Fax: 705-745-2326

Japan: Tuttle-Shokai, 21-13 Seki 1-Chome, Tama-ku,
Kawasaki, Kanagawa 214
Tel: 44-833-1924 Fax: 44-833-7559

A full catalogue is available on request.

ORDER FORM

(please photocopy if you do not wish to cut up your book)

TITLE *(please tick box)*	PRICE	QUANTITY	TITLE *(please tick box)*	PRICE	QUANTITY
☐ The Lusts Of The Libertines	£7.95		☐ Flesh Unlimited	£7.95	
☐ Dungeon Evidence	£9.95		☐ The Whip Angels	£4.95	
☐ The Velvet Underground	£7.95		☐ House Of Pain	£4.95	
☐ Whiplash Castle	£7.95		☐ Irene's Cunt	£7.95	
☐ The Snake	£7.95		☐ Psychopathia Sexualis	£9.95	
☐ The Black Rose	£7.95		☐ Torture Garden	£16.95	
☐ Philosophy In The Boudoir	£7.95		☐ Baby Doll	£12.95	
☐ The She Devils	£7.95		☐ City Of The Broken Dolls	£12.95	
☐ The Pleasure Château	£7.95		☐ Heat	£14.95	

Total Amount £_____ ☐ I enclose cheque/money order ☐ I wish to pay by ☐ Visa ☐ Mastercard

Card No: |___|___|___|___|___|___|___|___|___|___|___|___|___|___|___|___| Expiry_____

Signature_____Date_____

Name_____

Address_____

_____Telephone_____

Please add 10% to total price for postage & packing in UK (max. £5.00) 20% outside UK (max £10.00).
*Make cheques/money orders payable to **Velvet Publications** and send to 83 Clerkenwell Road, London EC1R 5AR (Sterling only)*

VELVET PUBLICATIONS